Living the Mystery

Living the Mystery

**Affirming Catholicism
and the Future of Anglicanism**

Edited by
JEFFREY JOHN

Introduction by
DAVID HUTT

DARTON·LONGMAN + TODD

First published in 1994 by
Darton, Longman and Todd Ltd
1 Spencer Court
140–142 Wandsworth High Street
London SW18 4JJ

ISBN 0–232–52071–2

A catalogue record for this book is available
from the British Library

Phototypeset by Intype, London
Printed and bound in Great Britain
by Page Bros, Norwich

Contents

Notes on Contributors

LAVINIA BYRNE IBVM is Associate Secretary for the Community of Women and Men in the Church (Council of Churches for Britain and Ireland).

FRANK T. GRISWOLD is Bishop of Chicago.

RICHARD HOLLOWAY is Bishop of Edinburgh and Primus of the Episcopal Church in Scotland.

DAVID HUTT is Vicar of All Saints, Margaret Street, London.

DAVID JENKINS is Bishop of Durham.

JEFFREY JOHN is Vicar of Holy Trinity, Eltham.

PHILIP SHELDRAKE SJ is a tutor at Westcott House, Cambridge, and General Editor of the Jesuit magazine, *The Way*.

STEPHEN SYKES is Bishop of Ely.

ANGELA TILBY is a writer, television producer and broadcaster.

ROWAN WILLIAMS is Bishop of Monmouth.

Introduction*

David Hutt

David Hare's successful play *Racing Demon* is a commentary on the Church of England. An anxious and despairing priest from an urban parish determines an atmosphere of crisis as soon as the curtain rises with his heartrending cry: 'God, where are you?'

The answer, unspoken, is that God is in the mess, the muddle, the confusion, and the doubt of that man. But God is also in other places and other life situations, which is not to deny his presence in all areas of our experience. As we become aware of the tension between belonging and not belonging, of reliance and betrayal, of knowing and not knowing, the significance of the Passion begins to dawn on us. But we have, in some small measure, to have *been there*. The encouragement derived from the Affirming Catholicism Conference held at York in the first week in September 1993 was once again about the people we really were and the stories we carried with us, evidence of the uniqueness and mystery, an affirmation that there was yet more to be discovered, more to be disclosed.

Interest in this compelling adventure is widespread and the evidence is there, not just among the 400 or so people (laity, religious, and clergy alike) who attended the conference hall each day, but in the oblique observation provided in novels and plays currently enjoying wide public acclaim. It may be supposed that this merely reflects a ghoulish fascination with death-bed scenes (or public executions?) when it comes to looking at the terminal

*© David Hutt 1993

1

decay and imminent demise of certain familiar customs, landmarks, and institutions. A more positive view will hold that the observant eye and ready pen of the playwright or novelist can help us to formulate necessary questions and express the pain and disillusionment which mark a time of transition from the old to the new. What may appear to be finality and what may feel like death is, in the Christian comprehension, the necessary prelude to life.

It now becomes clear that during the course of the past three or four years the movement known as 'Affirming Catholicism' has acted as a kind of catalyst in bringing people together from varied Christian backgrounds and positions within the church, and very many stages of life experience. The one recognizable and consistent factor which identifies those who have sought some kind of affiliation is a readiness to move and grow. This violition is the antithesis of that world-view which makes the Gospel and its proclamation a static event and a scripted programme.

Bearing this in mind, and in order to remain true to what brought some of us together in the early days, those of us who are part of this new movement have to recognize the limiting effect of becoming too institutionalized – yet another 'organization', another bureaucratic structure with no heart and no hands to hold and bless. Equally important is our willingness to let go and pass on, because the real significance of our affirmation must always be found at the point where an idea becomes rooted, where 'two or three are gathered together'. We set out to create nothing new, to offer nothing novel, because all things necessary were already in place, readily available, and simply waiting for the right moment for them to be taken up, given expression, grasped, and shared. I should like to explain what I think is beginning to be uncovered.

Recently I have been privileged to take part in a number of discussions and seminars with Lutheran Christians from the Church in Sweden who have visited London in search of 'the Anglican experience' (whatever that may be). The convenor of one such group invited me to speak on the theme 'Ancient Creed – Modern Man' in contravention of a previous agreement that we would be particularly sensitive in the area of inclusive language! Nevertheless, we accepted that a way into discussion was to examine the thesis that much of the time those with responsibility for proclamation were busy answering questions that no one was bothering to ask. A line of enquiry followed up in preparation for that particular seminar led me back to E. F. Schumacher's *Small is Beautiful*, where I rediscovered the words:

> It is hardly likely that twentieth-century man is called upon to discover truth that had never been discovered before. In the Christian tradition, as in all genuine traditions of mankind, the truth had been stated in religious terms, a language which has become well nigh incomprehensible to the majority of modern men. The language can be revised and there are contemporary writers who have done so while leaving the truth inviolate.[1]

Now, sad to relate, very many people seem to prefer the container to the contents, or even the earth which has long hidden the pearl of great price. Familiarity with the mellifluous and lovely language of Cranmer and the King James Version of the Bible may lead us to overlook the fact that English, as it is handed down, can become obscure, even though poetic, but more seriously misleading, since emphasis and interpretation change over the years.

Much theological language of whatever variety has little or no meaning of value because, in the words of John Lee, 'it has no clusters of associative intimacies with which to surround, and both the religious image and the religious idea lose all their power because of this false separation'.[2] The fly trapped in amber remains something remote, a novelty until it is surrounded by 'associative intimacies', the thinking, imagery and feelings that go to make up the perception that this insect, part of an evolving strain, is both known and commonplace yet it may carry something of the unknown by containing within itself data which

3

may yield up valuable scientific information. Our choice of what we put around any intimate object (or, for that matter, other people) says quite a lot about ourselves and the way in which we make use of stored-up associations, many of which have their origins far back in the past, and which may now have lost their significance and usefulness.

No one is really free of the influences of environment and cultural conditioning, and the way in which we accumulate our store of associations will depend very largely on circumstances outside ourselves. Sometimes the imposition of family mores, the influence of parents or teachers, the pressures imposed by religions can be so repressive that what we have come to recognize as unquestioning fundamentalism is the all too familiar outcome. The power of the cult leaders derives not directly from the force of their personalities but from the acquiescence of the cult members and the associations they bring within themselves to the whole area of authority. Sometimes, when faced with freedom of action or choice in quite simple processes of decision-making, the prospect of entering unknown territory is far more terrifying for individuals with no powers of association, no experience or knowledge, than the blind obedience which is at least familiar and reassuring.

By stepping outside the confines of conditioning it is possible for the individual to perceive new realities and come to a deeper understanding of what is truly present in the world rather than accept external evidence of the projections from within. All too often the institutionalized Church constructs as a basic strategy a language for the perpetuation of permanence. On the whole it does not encourage self-examination or self-enquiry, and it prefers to limit the vantage points and provide places of observation of which it approves. In demonstrating their protest, the valiant few have occasionally influenced the life of the Church for good by leaping the confining wall or, Zacchaeus-like, shinning up the metaphorical tree in order to gain new vision and call others to recognize the broad horizons. Any steps taken towards recovering the person who is empowered to examine the store of imposed or acquired associations involve risk, because they must entail the shedding of unnecessary luggage and the freedom and confidence to make new judgements and create new associations. This can mean a quite painful process of re-evaluation and self-identification in the face of all the influences that have come to bear during the course of a lifetime. It will affect long-held and treasured ideas, friendships, relationships, the positions held in hierarchies, the very notion of God.

Unless something like this process is undertaken, there will inevitably set in a degree of quiescence and stagnation, the very antithesis of the promise of Life in all its fullness and abundance. Any individual, structure, or institution committed to self-preservation and self-perpetuation cannot, in any sense, become a vehicle for striking out towards new goals. In particular, religious institutions tend to be fixed by cultural conditioning and a wholly stultifying weight of expectation imposed by their members and associates. One characteristic of this imposed association is an especial reverence for the past, and it really does appear sometimes that the past is sanctified and revered at the expense of the present and the future.

Not surprisingly, the game of providing answers before the questions are posed extends to the ministry of the Church and the way in which candidates for ordination training must come up against an agenda of expectation which channels them and their personhood into fixed runnels. For all the improved skills in interviewing and selection, the tramlines are laid down and, for those aspirants who risk telling their own stories, disclosing themselves and their associations, there is a real risk of rejection. As John Lee has said in his essay, 'there are those who cannot share their real and intimate souls for fear of being abandoned by the Church, which demands faith and not doubt, and by a God who punishes more often than he forgives'.[3] What we each bring to the proclamation of the Gospel in terms of our own associations is, in a real sense, a disclosure of ourselves. I am sometimes accused of reiterating

5

this view too frequently and too forcefully, but I believe passionately that the people we most truly *are* is the very best evidence for the Christian faith. Becoming the people we are intended to be is a lifetime's work and few can be sure of achieving more than a modicum of success in realizing the rich potential for fulfilment. Yet held in the mind's eye of the Creator is a unique and precious being, truly an icon of loving creation destined for life, liberty, and the work of freeing fellow human beings from the shackles of a dead past, irrelevant, destructive, and imperfect associations.

Our efforts at evangelism are rendered ineffective if we will not listen to and observe both ourselves and others. Really to hear demands stillness and receptivity, a willingness to suspend impulsive speech and the unnecessary sense of obligation to have something to say about everything under the sun. There is far too much talk, and the noise is deafening, drowning out the important questions and the cries for help: 'God, where are you?' And in reply, from I Kings 19:12, comes the answer: 'And after the wind, the earthquake; and after the fire, a still small voice . . .'

All that led up to us being together at York began with a rather British reaction to the no longer tolerable. Certain ridiculous things were happening and people were getting away with absurdities – in particular the kind of Anglo-Papalism that we refer to in a rather jokey way, but which is thoroughly corosive in its effects. Part of what we have done has been to prick the bubble of the fantasy that you can pretend to be a Roman Catholic in everything but obedience. For that reason we have found ourselves in an adversarial position and we cannot extricate ourselves from it. We are, of course, terribly nice people who are committed to consensus and 'getting it right', but there are points at which we have to be prepared to engage in conflict. By our protest we have drawn together a lot of people who have responded to the absurdities in a very positive way.

One group of fellow travellers consists of those who

have recently come into the Church, or who have looked at their commitment to their faith in a new way and realized their need for Catholicism's sacramental and spiritual riches. They have looked for the intellectual rigour which has been characteristic of the Anglican tradition for centuries, and have hungered for Catholic discipline. Perhaps they have read books by some of those who were speakers at York, or found themselves a spiritual director, a soul friend, or made a retreat, or joined a discussion group. They need nourishment: they are looking for the kind of Catholicism that we have to offer, which is not to be found elsewhere in our Anglican tradition. We have a duty to them.

There is another constituency which is more than mildly interested in our endeavour to build an open, confident and positive Catholicism. This is the much wider ecumenical field of European Catholicism, in which we find the roots and inheritance of our own. To take only one strand of common tradition, there is the great Benedictine family; how many Anglican travellers and seekers have ventured to the monasteries of Bec, Saint-Bénoît, Chèvetogne and Saint Wandrille de la Fontanelle, to find there is a sensible, uncluttered Catholicism, a down-to-earth liturgical offering ready and waiting? And how many European Catholics look to our present wrestlings and changes, not with contempt but with envy, hoping and yearning that they will be the prefiguring of their own?

In the same way we must extend an ecumenical hand of friendship to the Free Churches and to all our Protestant brothers and sisters, since we are, after all, a reformed Church as well as a Catholic Church. In the past we have been extremely aloof and snooty, but now we must give ourselves permission to learn from fellow Christians who are living a Catholic life, a life that is sometimes impressively deep and committed in a way that many members of the Anglican Church could hardly claim. So we can identify these two special groups – those who are looking up and needing to be fed; and those who can nourish us from their own tradition, if only we are prepared to recognize and acknowledge what they have to offer.

Since the beginning of Affirming Catholicism and the seminal gathering at St Alban's, Holborn, in June 1990 we have come close to identifying ourselves as creatures *in via*. As such we share a belief that our experience is of value to the life of the whole Church as part of a wider exploration into which we are all being drawn. Our hands are set to plough and there can be no going back. What we lack in definition and precise manifesto is made up for by a sense of truth and the conviction that we are somehow on the right road. It is for others, contemporary commentators and future historians, to evaluate success and failure; for ourselves, we are empowered in our strivings by the strength of conviction.

A letter from Fr Philip Sheldrake summarizes much of what has been contained in the correspondence following on from the 1993 conference. He expresses himself as being less sure about 'campaigns' but inclined instead towards the idea of 'safe places' where people may find space and opportunity to deepen their vision and to embrace change at their own pace and in God's good time. The following is reproduced with his permission:

> I very much appreciated the invitation to York and to join with you all in affirming a vision of Catholicity that I found encouraging and energizing. I confess that I was mildly apprehensive – simply because, despite positive noises from friends who already knew Affirming Catholicism, I did not know what I would meet. What I did encounter was not a Catholicism of exclusion (as in 'We are the only real Catholics') nor of the minutiae of ritual behaviour nor of some precious garden enclosed. There was a healthy vigour to the occasion and a vision that felt expansive and, as a friend said afterwards, 'grand' in its potential. I suppose that it is not really for me to make a plea for anything but, nevertheless, I shall! Firstly, I hope that Affirming Catholicism will always see itself as saying something about the Church and not about a party or group of like-minded people. Catholicity, it seems to me, is about finding

community and 'like-heartedness' at a deeper level than simply ways of worshipping or even of stating belief. Secondly, I hope that Affirming Catholicism will both be confidently Anglican (i.e. know where it comes from) rather than apologetically sub-Roman and, at the same time, be open to working with friends from other traditions (and, indeed, other national cultures) that come broadly under the Catholic umbrella. It needs an ecumenical and international flavour. Finally, I hope that the vision will continue to be broad and to address the critical religious, cultural, and social issues of our times. Affirming Catholicism can undoubtedly fill a vacuum within the Anglican tradition in these islands, but I think that if it plays its cards right it can also offer something energetic to an ecumenical situation that needs new energy and vision.

It is in this spirit that this volume has been compiled.

1 E. F. Schumacher, *Small is Beautiful*, Abacus, 1973, p. 248.
2 John Lee, 'Honest to What?' in E. James (ed.), *God's Truth*, SCM, 1988, p. 150.
3 ibid., loc. cit.

1 Towards Catholicity: Naming and Living the Mystery*

Frank T. Griswold

I am here not only as Bishop of Chicago, which is the largest of the historically Catholic dioceses in the American Episcopal Church, but also as one who has lived intimately with the reality of women in the priesthood for the past sixteen years. Yet I have to say that all that the Church has lived through and is living through, and all that I have lived through and am living through, has at the same time been profoundly consoling; and it is out of that consolation that I want to speak to you about naming and living the mystery of Catholicity in this uncertain and confusing time. I would like to ground us first of all in a text of Scripture, a passage from 2 Corinthians which has been very important to me over the years. 'Blessed be the God and Father of our Lord Jesus Christ, the Father of mercies and the God of all consolation, who consoles us in all our affliction, so that we may be able to console those who are in any way afflicted with the consolation with which we ourselves are consoled by God.' I really come to share the consolation which has come out of affliction, in the experience of being Bishop of Chicago and a bishop in the Episcopal Church in this curious season we have been passing through.

While serving as Rector of St Martin in the Fields in Philadelphia, I was able to share pastoral ministry with two exceptional women priests, one of whom I had the honour of baptizing as an adult, and travelling with as

*© Frank T. Griswold 1993

she went through the process of discerning a vocation to ordained ministry. This was immensely helpful to me in sorting out some of my initial ambivalence. I remember once being asked by a very intellectual community of Roman Catholic religious who ran a college in Chestnut Hill, if I would come and talk about women in the priesthood. I replied that the living manifestation of that reality would be a more effective witness than my opinion, and I was able to prevail upon my assistant to go with me. I remember how, at the end of her description of her journey to ordination, one of the older sisters in the room came forward with her eyes gleaming and said, 'That's it, it's all about vocation!' She was able to sense the intrinsic rightness of it, and I think that was very helpful to her sisters, as it was certainly a confirmation of rightness to me.

After 16 years of saying with Gamaliel, 'if it is of God it will endure', I am led to say that for me and for many others the intrinsic rightness of the ordination of women to priesthood is beyond question, as well as being altogether consistent with a Catholic understanding of ordained ministry. There are any number of poignant, disturbing, as well as heart-gladdening and amusing stories I could tell you about resistance to and acceptance of the ordination of women, not only in congregations and dioceses but also in communities of women religious. However, the overriding truth is that the whole matter is really a process of time and incarnation. The hypothetical becomes flesh, someone encounters the reality, someone who may well have been very resistant or unsure. They are confronted with a person who manifests quite clearly and unambiguously the charisma of Christ's own priesthood, and so often the response is, 'Well, of course, I can accept *you* and I can believe in *your* sacramental ministrations.' Then they hear themselves and realise what they have said, and the light dawns: 'Well, I guess if I can accept you I can accept all women priests.' And so the shift is made, if the shift is to be made at all. At this point after 16 years, 93 of the 98 domestic dioceses of the Episcopal Church welcome

11

the ministry of ordained women. The remaining five still resist it, but my sense is that over time reception will continue, and in the fullness of time – gracefully, I hope – those five dioceses will join the other 93.

Division and controversy in the Episcopal Church have been greatly exaggerated in the press. Certainly there are two or three rather volatile and vocal groups. They use mostly scare tactics, preying on people's fears, with suggestions such as 'If you ordain women you will be restoring goddess worship' and so on. I very seldom read what these organizations put out. This means that when I am asked in the course of a visitation what I think about what one or another of these groups has to say, I can reply with equanimity, 'I have no idea what they have to say. Please tell me.' Often the person asking the question cannot do so; all they do is to tell me that they have received a letter telling them in exaggerated and inflammatory terms that they should be upset and highly concerned about some issue or another.

I am also aware that the negative always weighs more heavily upon us and engages us more fully than does the positive. Our psychic energy is naturally entrapped, so to speak, by things that are negative, and so a disproportionate amount of energy goes into dealing with them or feeling their significance. One has to be very careful to try always to strive for balance, not discounting the negative voices, but remembering that these voices are not by any means the whole story. I am sure that many of you have had the experience of receiving ten positive letters, then one negative letter comes, and that one negative letter somehow cancels out the joy of the ten positive letters. That tells us something about the way we normally function, and so we have to be very careful and discerning in assessing the real strength of these objections and fears, and not allow ourselves to be pulled off course by them.

My conviction is that the ordination of women is a genuine development of doctrine carried out under the aegis of the Spirit, and not a sociological aberrancy. This was brought home to me quite wonderfully last December when I was *en route* from Jerusalem to Chicago, having completed ten weeks of a twelve-week sabbatical. I broke my journey in Rome for two purposes; one (the primary one) was to visit the newly refurbished rooms in which Ignatius of Loyola lived and died next to the Church of the Gesù. I have a particular fondness for Ignatius and have profited immensely from the Spiritual Exercises. I also thought that, as co-chair of the Anglican-Roman Catholic dialogue in the United States, I ought to call upon some of the personnel in the Office of Christian Unity. I had made arrangements to do precisely that, but when I arrived in Rome early in December I found that my visit had been, as it were, upgraded and I was now going to have a private audience with the Pope. I think this was because a few weeks earlier the Church of England had decided to advance the cause of the ordination of women to the priesthood, and I have a feeling that probably I was the first Anglican to visit the Vatican after that vote had been taken. So I found myself in the antechamber, gazing at a tiny El Greco, waiting for my turn to come. I was in the company of a Roman Catholic bishop who was waiting to make his *ad limina* visit to the Bishop of Rome (all Roman Catholic bishops are required to visit the Holy Father every five years and give a personal report as to the shape and direction of their ministry). This particular bishop, when I introduced myself as the Anglican Bishop of Chicago, said, 'Ah yes, the Church of England.' He then went on to say, 'There is absolutely no theological reason why women should not be ordained, and there is certainly every sociological reason why it should be done.' Then a curious smile played across his lips and I thought, 'Here it comes.' He said, 'But,' raising one finger, 'is it God's will?' I pondered for a moment and said, 'Well, you know, sometimes you only discover God's will by doing something, and it is in the actual doing of it that the intrinsic rightness or wrongness is revealed.' I pointed out that that was Gamaliel's principle, at which point a buzzer rang announcing that it was now his turn, and he went forth

13

into the papal study edified, I hoped, by his conversation with the Bishop of Chicago.

Then my turn came and I didn't quite know what to expect. I was taken through several more rooms into a study where a figure was sitting at a desk; the figure was, of course, dressed in white, and it jumped up and came towards me. I fell to my knees and kissed his ring. I have to confess (this may horrify some of you) that it was a completely unplanned and unpremeditated gesture on my part. I reflected on it later; 'Ah, Frank Griswold, something deep within you recognised the fact that this is the patriarch of the Western Church, even if you are not in communion with him.' In any event he helped me up, put me in a chair at the end of his desk, pulled his chair over, put his head in his hands and then shook his head and commented upon the difficulties posed by the Church of England's decision to ordain women to the priesthood. What that moment revealed to me was a certain sadness, but not the old insecurity about displeasing Rome nor a sense of apology, because at the same time I felt again that sense of the profound rightness of what you are preparing to do, and what we and other provinces of the Anglican Communion have done. Yes, there was a sadness that this is a further division, but one that I hope will be overcome in the fullness of time. I also reminded him gently that his predecessor's condemnation of Anglican orders in 1896, which has never been set aside, also posed difficulties. And so we sat and pondered difficulty from two perspectives. Later on he made mention of the inclusivity of Anglicanism. I allowed that that may be difficult for someone in his place and system, but said that I saw it very much as part of God's unique call to us. I did not say this next thing to him, but I should like to claim that I did (you know how oral tradition can improve a story). Had I thought of it I *would* have said, 'To my way of thinking, Anglicanism, is, as it were, "the least of the tribes of Israel" entrusted by God with this particular call: namely, to integrate women fully into the life of the Church. We can do it because we are a mixture of tradition and bold pragmatism, all of which is able to fit into a structure of inclusiveness and publicly accepted diversity. And if there is a milieu in which a shift such as the ordination of women in a Catholic structure might occur, then I think Anglicanism is probably best suited for that occurrence to take place.'

I have been a bishop for almost nine years, co-adjutor for three, and diocesan for almost six. There are probably more clergy and lay persons in the diocese of Chicago opposed to the ordination of women than in most American dioceses that allow women to be ordained. I live in full communion with all but one priest, who told me over lunch shortly after I became diocesan, 'Father, I like everything about you, you're just the kind of bishop this diocese needs, but I am afraid I can't be in communion with you because you will ordain women.' I replied, 'I rather thought it was my prerogative to determine matters of communion,' and he laughed and we had another glass of wine. Canonically he is resident in another diocese but is licensed to function in the diocese of Chicago, and we continue in all other respects to be in communion, and friends.

Increasingly, open acknowledgement of sexual self-expression other than in heterosexual marriage is becoming an issue in the life of the diocese of Chicago and other dioceses, and that issue (together with various other strains and stresses of church life, including the continuing reception of the ordination of women) often leaves me feeling beleaguered. I find a temptation to indulge in the slough of despond and to enjoy that dark and singularly immobilizing pleasure of self-pity. Poor Frank, so misunderstood, so unloved, so lonely! Mercifully, God has sent me truth-bearers who stand against some of that indulgence, including my wife, who gives very little space to these excursions into self-pity and pulls me up short. She did so one night when I woke up at 3.00 a.m., which is usually when the demons set upon me. (Possibly some of you are familiar with the demons who come at 3.00 a.m. when your worries break fully upon you in their most

15

drastic and catastrophic form.) So there I was, moaning and fussing, pretending that I was only moaning and fussing to myself, but hoping that I might wake up the form sleeping beside me so that she might offer solace. Finally one eye opened and a tired voice said, 'Is something wrong?' and I said, 'This is going to kill me, this being a bishop is going to kill me,' and the sleepy voice said, 'Isn't that what it is all about?' and the eye shut, and she went back to sleep, and so did I, convicted and released.

On my sabbatical I stood one day at the edge of the Jordan Valley contemplating a monastic cave of the fifth century cut into the cliff above a wadi, and I found myself swept away by thoughts of the incredible asceticism and discipline that had led people to live in that remote place. As I stood there, a voice within my mind said, 'Frank, all the asceticism you need is in Chicago.' I felt deeply consoled and ready to return home to whatever was being revealed. I realized that my own cave in the wilderness is a very public place, and yet the struggles are very much the same.

When I was ordained a bishop it was the custom to produce some sort of memorial card which is handed out to commemorate the event. Usually people choose icons or representations of something properly sacred printed in Italy, but I decided to do something more severe and Quakerly since I came from Philadelphia, so I had brown cards printed that have at the top a mother pelican biting her breast to feed her young, which I chose to remind me of the maternal dimensions of episcopal ministry. Below it is a quotation from the great Brazilian bishop Helder Camara. I chose this quotation in all innocence, thinking it was quite lovely but having no idea what it might mean along the way. It goes like this: 'The bishop belongs to all. Let no one be scandalized if I frequent those who are considered unworthy or sinful. Let no one be alarmed if I am seen with compromised and dangerous people on the left or the right. Let no one bind me to a group. My door, my heart must be open to everyone, absolutely everyone.' What has become clear nine years later is that this is no

16

easy task. Yet it is very much God's demand in the concrete reality of episcopal ministry, particularly when various factions try to co-opt you and become enraged when you show what from their perspective is undue sympathy for people on the other side of some issue. And I need to say here that, though I see myself very much in a progressive camp, I am appalled at how rigid and condemnatory people who are progressive can also be towards others. In many instances their rancour is far worse than some of the uncharity that comes from conservative or traditional quarters. In any event, episcopal ministry means trying to live out those words of Helder Camara, and I have a long way to go.

I come here to share a consolation that has come out of affliction; and I see consolation not as an emotion, but as Ignatius defines it: 'an increase of faith, hope and love' beyond self-satisfaction or self-congratulation; a place of faith, hope and love that leaves us active and open to others, that grounds us in courage and that makes us able to endure. I come here recognising that you as an ecclesial household are going through your own season of affliction.

In the United States some members of the clergy who describe themselves as standing in the Catholic tradition have lost heart and slipped into desolation, often abetted by an abandonment of prayer. They go through the motions, supported by the structures of the Prayer Book and the ecclesial system, waiting for retirement, just hanging on. Paradoxically, many Catholic battles appear to have been won in terms of external signs and patterns of worship, as our 1979 Prayer Book makes very clear. Yet there is often at the same time a profound sense of loss, and I have tried to figure out what that comes from. I think it comes partly from a great many Catholic-minded people needing to feel *singular*, and resenting in a way the fact that the Prayer Book has now countenanced, approved, and opened some of the things they used to consider their special prerogatives and insights. Once every parish has a shrine of Our Lady of Walsingham in the north aisle it is not so much fun! And then there is the

17

question: Is Anglican Catholicism, as a distinct perspective, a grain of wheat which must die, or has died, in order to bear much fruit; and if so, what is the fruit it has borne? Some mourn the loss of what I can only call gnostic superiority, the warm feeling that we possess by virtue of our Catholicism, a greater truth, *the* Catholic truth which allows us to look with a certain disdain on those who prefer to remain in darkness and the shadow of death. Another shift which has created or contributed to this sense of loss is a new understanding or an enriched understanding of what it means to be ordained. The Tractarians, God bless them, put heavy emphasis on apostolic succession as a guarantee of the divine legitimacy of the Church and the sacraments, but this has given way to a more dynamic and less static understanding of ordained ministry, in which the emphasis falls more on 'apostolic' than it does on 'succession' – more on the content of faith and doctrine than the mechanics of hierarchy.

The incorporation of women in that ministry has changed our notions of tradition as something fixed and given. No longer can we say (if we ever really could say it honestly in the first place) that we hold *quod semper ubique et ab omnibus*; more and more we are invited to look forward and see tradition as something dynamic and unfolding, always being re-formed and brought into being. Change, the American philosopher Eric Hoffer once observed, is always experienced as loss, even when we welcome it intellectually. Change is always disorienting, and sometimes we mask our anxiety by manic enthusiasm for something, or we become a little prickly, or we lose our sense of humour; and all these may be tip-offs to the fact that the change is not being assimilated as easily as we might think it is. I know, for instance, much as I was in favour of revising Eucharistic rites and could explain all the whys and wherefores of what our new Prayer Book sought to do, that for at least a year I was disoriented celebrating the new rites; the rhythms didn't fit the way the rhythms of the old Prayer Book did, and I finally admitted, 'Frank, you're grieving. It does not mean that you want to go back to the old but you might as well admit that you are going through some grief. Don't try to hide it or you can't grow beyond it.'

What has collapsed within the Catholic tradition, at least in the United States, is certitude and we have entered into a period of disillusionment. The loss of certitude and entry into the dark night of disillusionment has been for me, and I believe for many others, an immense grace, an incredible blessing. It has given us the ability in a new way to pray with the psalmist, 'It is good for me that I have been afflicted, that I might learn your statutes,' and here 'statutes' means the truth, the reality, the passionate love of God. Or put another way, the loss of certitude has made much more real the dynamic truth of the paschal mystery that we find our life by losing it. And I need to say to you that while we tend often to think of the paschal mystery in highly personal terms, *my* dying and *my* rising, the paschal mystery also applies to our corporate life. Corporately we go through seasons of death and resurrection, and it is very important that we name them accurately when they occur and do not try to hide them, because if we try to hide them we will not discover the grace that those seasons of dying can reveal to us. Father Kelly, the founder of SSM, said, 'The opposite of faith is not doubt but certainty.' This same truth has been more amply unfolded by an American scholar, Walter Brueggemann, a professor of the Old Testament in St Louis, who has observed that the Bible 'is not about certitude but about truth which is made available to us only as narrative'. You can only live the truth over time as history, as something you experience. 'Truth comes relentlessly packaged in ambiguity, inscrutability, polyvalence.' Furthermore, he adds, 'our truth always comes with scars.' There is always suffering to be gone through.

The loss of certitude opens us to truth in new ways and so does disillusionment. Parker Palmer, a Quaker theologian in the United States, observes that disillusion literally strips us of our illusions about life, about others, about ourselves, and makes us permeable to God's truth and

19

God's reality in new ways. He also speaks about 'dislocation, in which our angle of vision suddenly changes and we see from a new perspective, a perspective which may confront us with a strange and threatening landscape'. I think some of what we are going through is indeed a strange and threatening landscape. The answer, Jesuit spirituality says again and again, is to be found in the pain of living fully what is going on; but of course our tendency is to avoid or resist the pain and, as I said earlier, thereby miss the lesson that the pain, the suffering, the struggle, might be able to teach us. Desolation is its own word. Desolation is a wonderful teacher, and what we need to do is to question it and ask, what is it you are trying to speak to me? Consolation emerges from that querying of desolation. The consolation that has emerged from me comes from facing the fact that I am in many ways in a place of desolation, a place of dislocation. The consolation is that I am in the wilderness, the Church is in the wilderness, and instead of resenting that condition we need to welcome it. The desert is not simply a place but an experience of vulnerability, poverty, limitations, and also a place where we experience God. Origen, in speaking of the desert, once said, 'the air is purer, the sky more open, and God is closer'. And Charles de Foucauld, the great modern father of the desert, observed, 'Il faut passer par le désert et y séjourner pour recevoir la grâce de Dieu,' you have to pass through the desert and stay there for a *long* time in order to receive the grace of God. So what has become very helpful to me is to reflect upon the wilderness journey of the children of Israel as a paradigm of what we are going through as a community of faith. The first thing that strikes me is: 'Why forty years, O God?' Why couldn't it all have been accomplished in one dazzling moment, taking all the children of Israel out of Egypt, transporting them through the air and landing them by nightfall in the promised land? Again and again I hear people saying, 'Why do we have to go through this, why does it have to be so murky and obscure and convoluted and paradoxical?' I am sure that many who made that journey through the wilderness asked the same sorts of questions, and had the same sorts of responses. The answer is that we need the desert because the desert forms us; it is not simply something to be got through, it is part of living into the new reality that lies on the other side. An American theologian said, 'The children of Israel needed to go through the wilderness for forty years in order to be prepared for freedom,' in order to be prepared to receive the land of promise as a gift. So I say to myself, I don't understand all that is going on, I wish the Church from the outside looked more sensible, more orderly, more clear about what it was doing; yet on the other hand I trust that all this has a purpose which will be revealed in the fullness of time. The desert is a place of purification, of being stripped down, and it is out of that being stripped down that the new awareness, the new sense of self, the new freedom can emerge. Along with this I note that Israel travels through the wilderness by stages. There is a homily by Origen on that fact, in which he points out that the stages represent spiritual development. He notes that at the beginning of Numbers 33 each of the places at which they arrive and from which they depart are mentioned twice, as a point of arrival and as a point of departure, in order to underscore the fact that each place is part of that integral journey. You can't skip over two places in order to get to the third. And so each thing we are living is integral and important, and we need to be profoundly present to each moment along the way and not allow resentment, or bitterness, or impatience to overtake us.

Then in the wilderness the children of Israel had the experience of manna. Manna which came to them at a moment of complete desperation and absolute poverty and powerlessness. At first they did not recognize it, they did not know that it was food. They said, 'What on earth is this ghastly stuff?' until one of them tasted it, and said 'It's not bad, it might be something we can actually eat.' And this is the way grace often breaks upon us in the wilderness. It doesn't come in ways that are easy to discern. Grace in the wilderness comes in surprising ways,

21

ways that catch us off guard, and so in order to be faithful to the journey through the wilderness we have to be ready to be surprised by the various ways in which manna comes to us. It can be the word of another person, it can be simply a look, it can be something we read, it can be all sorts of things, but the purpose of it is to give us the courage, the ability, to go on and remain faithful. The other thing about manna is that you can't store it up. Only once were the children of Israel allowed to store up the manna and that was in order to have enough for the Sabbath, but when they tried to store it at other times it turned sour and foul. In the same way you can't cling to grace, you can't say, 'I'll get all this consolation here and now, and that will get me through whatever lies ahead.' God gives us enough for each moment, provided we accept the grace of each moment.

Then there is the golden calf, which simply represents to me the need for certitude when we panic. You remember how Moses goes up into the mountain and into the cloud, and the children of Israel don't know what to do; they need some focus, and so they make the golden calf. And I find myself asking, what are the golden calves I strike for myself, what symbols of certitude do I erect in my own wildernesses of insecurity rather than live through the insecurity relying upon God's grace alone? We need to be very careful how we deal with our need for certitude. We need to ask, are we turning certain things that ought to lead beyond themselves into something fixed and absolute that stops us rather than leading us on?

Then, of course, there is nostalgia. We remember the fleshpots, the cucumbers, the melons, the leeks, the Manual of Catholic Devotion, the first edition of Ritual Notes, the folded chasuble and all those other things which, if you put them in context alongside other things that are less lovely, make it perfectly clear we really don't want to go back to Egypt. Yet selectively we pick out certain things that draw us back rather than forward, we forget slavery and forced labour in all its subtle forms. We need to be careful about nostalgia.

22

Another thing one learns from the wilderness (and I think parish clergy and bishops are very aware of this one) is about murmuring. The children of Israel in the wilderness complained, 'Give us water, why did you bring us out here to kill us?' All their anger is projected on to Moses: 'You're responsible for this situation, this uncertainty, this disillusionment, this unknowing, all the changes we have had to go through.' Then Moses turns around and gives it to God. This resembles what happens often, at least in the United States, to those in episcopal ministry – which is possibly why so many of them wear lavender shirts so that they can be clear targets for all sorts of murmurings which get projected on to them. And of course in Scripture, where else should Moses turn? He has to murmur against God and there it stops, and God must be trusted to act. But be careful about murmuring. We all need to watch it; I come from a murmuring diocese and a murmuring church. It is a clear sign of being in the wilderness and of an unwillingness to live the journey faithfully.

Those are some thoughts about the wilderness that have been helpful to me. But then there is the promised land, which for me is the symbol of Catholicity, Catholicity meaning not simply something that is universal, but that which is whole and complete, that which makes something full, that which supplies totality. Father Benson once said, 'No age suffices to present to our view the Church of God in all its completeness.' Catholicity is something towards which we are moving, that we do not yet possess. Yet Catholicity has to be given a focus, otherwise it remains a kind of cosmic diffusion or whatever we might define it to mean. And clearly the focus of Catholicity is the person of Christ. Christ is the living fullness of God, active in the world, for in him we are told in Colossians, 'the whole fullness of deity dwells bodily, and you have come to fullness in him who is the head of every ruler and authority'. Again, from the opening chapter of John's Gospel, 'From his fullness (the fullness of Christ), we have all received grace upon grace.' It becomes the office of the Holy Spirit to take what belongs to Christ, the fullness of Christ, declare it, reveal it, work it into our lives. The Spirit unfolds that fullness of God which dwells in Christ by extending the Incarnation and continuing to give flesh to God's fullness in the concrete realities and struggles of our lives. There are no abstractions in this kind of Catholicity, this kind of fullness, no flying away on the wings of a dove. You have to stay put and there it is: incarnation in all its ambiguous, unclear, unsettling confusion. If you look at the Incarnation in Holy Scripture, what a mess, what a way for God to bring God's Word into the world; Joseph wondering by whom was Mary pregnant and wanting to put her away; why did God make it so confusing and allow it to be open to misunderstanding? But that is somewhat the way incarnation works in real life. Being a bishop has been for me an experience of incarnation. People will come up to me and say, 'Oh, we are so sorry that you can't just be a pastor, that you have to deal with administration.' I have learnt by now to say that administration is part of the pastoral office. If I have to fire the money managers of the diocesan endowment because of their poor performance and bring in a whole new raft from the West Coast, that is not administration, that's pastoral ministry, just as much as my caring for a priest in distress, just as much a matter of incarnation. Fullness of Catholicity is lived in the muck and muddle, not always safely anchored on a prie-dieu, not always gazing at the door of a tabernacle, though there are moments when both those things are necessary. Also the Spirit who ministers Catholicity creates Christ's fullness within us by breaking down the dividing walls of hostility in all their subtle and obvious forms, in us and between us. Part of fullness is to undo all that separates, all that works against the wholeness of authentic Catholicity, and that is why justice is integral to any notion of Catholicity, any notion of fullness, the fullness of Christ. Listen again to Father Benson: 'We must bear the pain of expansion, we are stretched indeed not on the rack of human torture but on the glorious being of the Holy Ghost.' It's a wonderful quotation from someone who knew whereof he spoke; that's not the kind of image that someone safe in piosities would come up with. The dynamic of Catholicity, of course, is the inner life of the Trinity, it is that love which is expressed, as Von Balthasar said, in 'an eternal dance of dispossession', whereby the three persons give themselves to each other and draw us into the dance. I am so glad that the Rublev icon of the Trinity is here. We stand on the fourth side of that icon and are drawn into it, drawn into Catholicity as fullness and justice, having all our walls of division broken down in order that we might be the incarnation of Christ's own fullness. And this love which is the life of the Trinity is experienced by us as mercy, it is through mercy that God overtakes us with his fullness, and mercy draws us in, mercy embraces us and, as it embraces us, mercy does something quite wonderful to us. Mercy gives us merciful, that is, Catholic hearts. But what is a merciful and Catholic heart? Isaac of Syria has the answer:

> It is a heart which burns with love for the whole of creation, for humankind, for the birds, for the beasts, for the demons, for every creature. When persons with a heart such as this think of the creatures and look at them their eyes are filled with tears and overwhelming compassion makes their heart grow small and weak and they cannot endure to hear or see any suffering, even the smallest pain inflicted upon any creature. Therefore they never cease to pray with tears even for the irrational animals, for the enemies of truth, for those who do them evil, asking that those for whom they pray may be guarded and receive God's mercy; and for the reptiles also they pray with a great compassion which rises up endlessly in their heart until they shine again and are glorious like God.

This is the Catholic heart, this is what this entire enterprise of Catholicity is about. It is not a position, it is something we live profoundly, it is something which changes us totally, and it is much more than psychological effort or active imagination. Living as we do in a time of intense bitterness and anger within the Church and within society generally, we can't survive and acquire Catholicity of heart by ourselves, and this is why prayer is so immensely important. It is prayer, as the late John Main defined it out of his years of deep contemplative praying, which opens us to love on every level of our being. Prayer makes possible a capacity for fullness, a permeability that allows Catholicity to overtake us and enter the secret place of our heart. Prayer overturns the idols, the golden calves which we erect; prayer is the work of the Spirit praying in us; it doesn't super-add something but rather purifies, clarifies, and deepens the word already planted within us. In one sense we don't pray, we give ourselves over to the Spirit who prays in us, and to find what this prayer consists of one can't do better than turn to *Four Quartets*, where Eliot speaks of Prayer, Observance (meaning the liturgy, the Church's year, the whole sacramental life) and Discipline (meaning constant metanoia, constant conversion and transformation and deepening). It is through prayer that we open ourselves to God's mercy and it is through prayer that we are given the gift of a merciful heart.

Yet Catholicity does not end there; because a merciful heart gives us something else, and that something else is what the New Testament calls simply boldness, boldness of speech. Boldness of speech comes from mercy, deeply received, deeply integrated, and then shared with others. Boldness of speech has nothing to do with cleverness, boldness has to do with a kind of frankness, plainness of speech, an outspokenness that is gentle, graceful, grounded, secure, not egotistical. Boldness of speech is clear, centred and confident. Athanasius describes Anthony coming out of his twenty-year sojourn in a derelict fortress where he has fought the demons, and says that Anthony had grace of speech which allowed those at enmity with one another to be reconciled; that is boldness of speech, a Catholic heart expressing itself. That is what God is seeking to work in us if we will allow him to have his way with us.

There is one final thing I want to share with you. This comes from a letter written on the occasion of the Easter Vigil in 1937 and the letter is found in a novel called

Mariette in Ecstasy. It is a book written by an American named Ron Hanson. The author of the letter is a woman who has suffered great affliction. She has experienced God's fullness as Christ's mercy and has lived a quiet and seemingly unexceptional life of prayer, observance, discipline, thought, and action, which amounts to a radical process of incarnation. In the letter she writes to the new prioress of the nearby convent where she herself had once been a novice. To me this is the most marvellous expression of so much of what I have been attempting to say. Mariette writes, 'We try to be formed and held and kept by [Christ], but instead he offers us freedom; and now when I try to know his will, his kindness floods me, his great love overwhelms me, and I hear him whisper, "Surprise me".'

As Catholic Christians in the Anglican tradition my prayer is that we may gratefully receive all that Christ offers us, the fullness of his mercy which is the ground of our freedom. I pray also that our hearts may be rendered open and merciful, that our speech may be bold, and that we may indeed accept Christ's challenge: 'Surprise me'.

2 Foundations of an Anglican Ecclesiology*

Stephen Sykes

Sitting in the meeting of Affirming Catholicism called at the York Synod in July 1993, listening to the Dean of Exeter, I was suddenly struck by the extraordinary and perhaps unperceived importance of what we were doing. The first thing I want to say is that, despite the sometimes absurd pretentiousness of established English Anglicanism, it is not negligible in world Christianity for there to be a Church in England, claiming to be the Catholic Church of the English nation, going about its ordinary business of preaching and teaching the Catholic faith and celebrating the Catholic sacraments. It is only ignorant parochialism which pretends that there is something disgracefully disqualifying about the fact of our current disagreements and arguments – as compared with the supposed unanimity which obtains in all the serious churches. On the contrary. I have come to the conclusion that, despite our smallness, something quite important in world Christian terms depends upon our living a quiet and confident Catholicism, which does not posture, strive or cry, which is serious about its prayer and self-discipline, which is energetic in its social witness, which understands secularity and accepts the obligation of honest evangelism, and which draws upon the intellectual and spiritual riches of the whole Catholic tradition.

I think it is undeniable that part of the importance of this movement derives from the anxious conservatism

*© Stephen Sykes 1993

28

of the current leadership in Rome. There are many Roman Catholics, I know, who look to Anglicans to embody this confident Catholicism, not least in relation to women's ministry, but also in its continuing receptivity to, and testing of, good argument in biblical and theological scholarship. I hope this will be *one* of the strands of Affirming Catholicism, without of course allowing the movement to become a talking shop or mobile study group, but as a proper expression of that proper celebration and offering of the intellect which has always been a feature of Catholic faith. It is in that spirit that I want to offer a paper on Anglican ecclesiology, which has *one* presupposition and *three* points to make:

The presupposition is that there must be an *Anglican ecclesiology*; that is, that Anglicans cannot take their doctrine of the Church second-hand and unadapted from other sources.

The three points are:

(i) That the Church is a visible sign of God's activity in human history.
(ii) That we have at all costs to keep contact with a sophisticated account of the understanding of the Church in the New Testament.
(iii) That the theology of baptism is foundational.

Since the General Synod's vote in November 1992 in favour of ending the rule restricting the priesthood to males, a great deal has been said about the Church of England in relation to Christ's One Holy Catholic and Apostolic Church which is frankly better forgotten. But the subject itself is anything but ephemeral, and there are some important perspectives from systematic theology to be brought to bear in a more than opportunistic or political way.

The Anglican doctrine of the Church

First, I should want to re-emphasize the importance of realizing that Anglicans have an obligation to develop a doctrine of the Church. There is no such thing as a generalized 'Catholic' theology of the matter. This is the conclusion one must draw from an even cursory appreciation of modern Orthodox ecclesiological writing, for example John Zizioulas's *Being as Communion* (1985), and the response of Professor Oliver Clement to 'Some Aspects of the Church as Communion', a letter to the Bishops of the Catholic Church from the Congregation for the Doctrine of the Faith (1992). At crucial points, notably on the subject of the relationship between the local and the universal Church, Orthodox and Roman Catholic theologies simply part company, and these are points on which Anglicans are bound to have rather different sympathies and interests. As a consequence they cannot take over either Orthodox or Roman Catholic ecclesiology without significant modifications.

A single example will make this point, relating to the papacy. In the recent Letter to the Bishops of the Catholic Church from the Congregation for the Doctrine of Faith ('Some Aspects of the Church as Communion', 1992) it is apparent that the papacy is being presented in the document on the Church as Communion as the logically prior interior principle of unity in the church: 'The ministry of the successor of Peter as something interior to each particular Church is a necessary expression of that fundamental mutual interiority between universal and particular Church' (para. 13). The argument had earlier been spelled out in an article by Cardinal Ratzinger entitled, 'The papal primacy and the unity of the people of God' (in *Church, Ecumenism and Politics* (1987)). Here it is asserted that it belongs inherently to the faith that the confession of Christ by the Church is as a community in which particular named persons bear personal responsibility. So Christian unity is represented in personalized form by Peter.

In his new name that transcends the historical individual

Peter becomes the institution which passes through history (since this ability of this institution to continue and the fact that it has continued is contained in this re-naming), but in such a way that this institution can only exist as a person and in personal responsibility tied to a particular name. (p. 36)

In this way theological anthropology is made to undergird the theology of primacy, so that the very act of confessing the faith entails what one might call a papal presupposition. 'Thus even when the claims of his office are disputed the pope remains a point of personal reference in the world's sight for the responsibility he bears and expresses for the word of faith' (p. 44). The point being made is an important one. To put it in the form of a negation, it proposes that papal primacy should not be regarded as an extrinsic addition to conciliar fellowship. It wants to connect desire for the unity of the Church, which is implicit in the personal profession of faith, with the focal character of the papacy – an understandable apologetic aim, even if there are major gaps, and dangers, in the precise formulation of the argument. At the very least, however, Anglicans who apparently figure in the Congregation's document among 'those ecclesial communities which have not retained the apostolic succession and a valid eucharist' (para. 17) would be obliged to recast their understanding of the Church in a fundamentally different way.

The same is true in relation to the ecclesiologies of the modern Protestant churches. Again the reason can be given very briefly. The episcopate in Anglicanism, though individual Anglican theologians have given differing accounts of it, has none the less functioned practically in such a way as to inhibit the growth of mutually tolerant recognitions of ministries. As a consequence, it is simply impossible to pass off a Reformed or Methodist doctrine of the Church as an Anglican one.

From both these examples I conclude that Anglican theologians have an inescapable responsibility to think through and to teach a doctrine of the Church. The present situation

31

reveals this fact with painful clarity. There are still those who call for an account of authority in the Church, as though that could be provided apart from a doctrine of the Church, or who treat priesthood and episcopate as though these ministries were not rooted in the nature of the Church itself. None of this is remotely adequate to the case, and we have been badly served by those Anglican theologians who in the past have assured their all-too-willing public that 'Anglicans have no doctrines of their own'. These have included some of our most venerated names. And while it may have been true that there is no specifically Anglican christology or doctrine of the Trinity, or even (though it could be disputed) doctrine of justification, it cannot be the case that there is no Anglican ecclesiology.

Some of us may be inclined to ask, how then have we been living all these years, convinced that we had no need of any such doctrinal support? The answer is instructive. It is perfectly possible for a Church to live out of the resources of what might be called an 'ecclesial instinct'. Explicit doctrine comes into its own in two situations, those of primary evangelism and of serious conflict. We need a doctrine of the Church at the present for both of these purposes. Men and women who come into new contact with the faith require a presentation of the nature of the Church appropriate to their situation. This must include an interpretation of conflict in the Church, and a way of living with the fact that Christians differ from each other. It will be part of my argument that the Anglican instinct on this matter is much clearer and more persuasive than we sometimes give ourselves credit for.

There is a further answer to the question of our apparently miraculous doctrineless survival, which is that we have, in fact, been far from inactive. There has been throughout the twentieth century a series of Anglican writers attending to ecclesiology, which has included Charles Gore, H. B. Swete, Norman Quick, Lionel Thornton, E. L. Mascall, F. W. Dillistone, Norman Pittinger, Stephen Neill and Michael Ramsey. More recently Paul

Avis has provided very helpful studies of the ecclesiologies of the English reformers and of later Anglicanism, as well as making contributions in his own right, and Tim Bradshaw has put us in his debt with a wide-ranging and irenic study of varieties of Anglican ecclesiologies in *The Olive Branch* (1992). If only the profundity of much of this effort were more evident in the public discourse of the Church, we would be less despondent. As it is, the slogan and the sound bite have achieved an altogether too great ascendency in our habits of speech and thought, and it is past time for us to dig deeper.

The Church as visible sign

A great deal of Western European theology since the Reformation, and especially since the European Enlightenment, has been developed on the assumption of a fundamental dichotomy between 'Catholic' and 'Protestant' principles. Friedrich Schleiermacher, the so-called 'father of modern theology', neatly encapsulated the alternative movement of faith either through the Church to Christ (the Catholic principle), or through Christ to the Church (the Protestant principle). The natural geographical context for such formulations is, of course, Germany, Holland, and Switzerland, where Catholic and Protestant communities live side by side. Contemporary ecumenism still produces a similar discussion about the existence of 'fundamental disagreements'.

Both the Orthodox and Anglicans are generally treated as marginal to this discussion. Anglicans, in particular, may feel themselves uncomfortable with the terms of the alternative. What, for example, do they make of the question whether the Church is fundamentally and essentially visible in character? This is the question refined by centuries of Roman Catholic apologetic with a view to embarrassing Protestants. The Catholic tradition is to give an unequivocally affirmative answer, and to point to the Roman Catholic Church as its exemplification. Protestants, on the other hand, are supposed to believe that the true

Church is invisible, because its extent is known only to God who alone can interpret a believer's faith. 'Church' occurs as and when God's promises and the summons to faith are offered in word and sacrament. In terms of their structures there can be many Churches, which can enjoy harmonious but autonomous membership in the One Church. Little justice though such an account does to more recent exposition of the ecclesiology of Luther or Calvin, such is popularly supposed to be the opinion of Protestantism. As a consequence it is polemically dismissed as 'individualistic'.

So much of the doctrine of the Church in the Western tradition has been argued out through the distorting lens of late medieval canon law, both in affirmation and negation, that it is a necessity to refer, time and again, to the Eastern tradition for the sake of balance and new insight. Under the subheading 'the "iconic" character of the ecclesial institutions', John Zizioulas argues for the importance of eschatology to all interpretation of the institutional character of the Church, including tradition, apostolic succession, scriptual foundation or actual historical needs. The Holy Spirit points beyond history, and as a result institutions become sacramental, losing their self-sufficiency, and existing *epicletically* (that is, they depend for their efficacy on prayer, the prayer of the 'community').

> It is not in history that the ecclesial institutions find their certainty (their validity) but in constant dependence on the Holy Spirit. This is what makes them 'sacramental', which in the language of Orthodox theology may be called 'iconic'. (p. 138)

To return to the blunt question of whether the Church is essentially visible or invisible, it turns out to be no mere evasion to say that it is both; and to insist (in Orthodox language) on the iconic character of its historical institutions and forms. We can go further. The dichotomy between visible and invisible is precisely one of those dualities or oppositions which are full of ambiguity, and which appear to require their own opposites. The Church's visibility is the necessary appearance in history of its

34

beyond-historical character, to which it points. While it is not complete or perfect in its historicality, neither is its historical being inessential or lacking in instrumental power. The visible signs are never self-sufficient, but always and only effective in the context of prayer and by the action of the invisible Spirit, who both governs and gives life to the Church and is therefore its Lord.

We may well prefer the category 'sign' to that of sacrament or icon because it is a biblical way of speaking of Jesus' own ministry, especially in the fourth Gospel. As C. H. Dodd has pointed out, for the writer of the fourth Gospel there is no reason why a narrative should not be at the same time factually true and symbolic of a deeper truth.

> Whilst in the first intention the feeding of the multitude signifies the timeless truth that Christ, the eternal Logos, gives life to men, and the healing of the blind that He is the Bearer of light, yet in the development of the argument we discover that Christ's work of giving life and light is accomplished, in reality and actuality, by the historical act of his death and resurrection. In that sense, every *semeion* (sign) in the narrative points forward to the great climax. (*The Interpretation of the Fourth Gospel* (1953), p. 142)

This conclusion is fully consistent with recent work on the sectarian background to the fourth Gospel's sacramentalism. Being baptised represents the threshold between the world and the community for John, as the believer publicly confesses allegiance to Christ as Son of God come down from heaven. The Eucharist reinforces the boundary this creates between believer and non-believer, and at the same time builds up solidarity between those who faithfully abide in Jesus. The 'sacraments' of baptism and Eucharist count as signs precisely because they point to the Passion of Christ and to the Resurrection. Together with Jesus' miraculous deeds (which continue in the experience of St Paul, see 2 Corinthians 12:12, 1 Corinthians 2:4, Romans 15:19) these signs are part of the reality of divine sovereignty in history (see Luke 11:20). They are thus likewise eschatological and inseparably linked to the presence and activity of the Spirit. The Church fundamentally belongs to the sign-character of God's activity in human history.

Interpreting biblical ecclesiology

To understand the Church as visible sign helps us to interpret the multiple images of ecclesia in the New Testament. The astonishing profusion of metaphors and images from previous theology and ordinary experience which go to make up New Testament ecclesiology has frequently been studied, notably by Paul Minear. His classic *Images of the Church in the New Testament* (1960) identifies no fewer than 96 images or analogies. Fortunately there is something close to a consensus that four images are dominant, namely:

  (i) 'the people of God';
 (ii) 'the body of Christ';
(iii) 'the communion of faith, hope, and love'; and
(iv) 'the creation of the Spirit'.

Each of these has an irreducible contribution to make to the historic development of the classic ecclesiologies of the major traditions. The 'people of God' is an image which establishes Christianity's continuity with Israel, and embodies the essential narrative reference characterizing the raw material of all Christian theology. Ecclesiology has always to be related to the specific experience of a concrete people in history, acting within the context of the covenant of God, whether in obedience or disobedience. The 'body of Christ' derives its power as an image from the crucifixion, death and resurrection, and is the natural vehicle for much of the sacramental mysticism of the Church's teaching. It is, therefore, intimately connected to the third of the images, that of a unity which is a social and ethical sharing in a common life. The three gifts of faith, hope, and love require and support each other, but it is love which binds everything and everyone together and completes the whole. Finally, the Church is the consequence of the activity of God's Holy Spirit, and there are a whole series of remarkable images of building a house or temple out of an assembly of persons.

In Ephesians 2 all the images are gathered together in a remarkable synthesis.

> The new *people of God* is not to exist at enmity with the old; both peoples are to be incorporated into *a single body* founded on the flesh and blood of Christ. This body is a true *communion*, in which there are no longer aliens and strangers but fellow citizens, members of God's household. And the bond or matrix of this building, household, temple, is the redemptive presence, the indwelling, the upbuilding, creative work of God as *Spirit*. (Hodgson, p. 34)

Inevitably the very richness and profusion of the metaphors and images have given rise to controversy, as one way of envisioning that the Church has achieved interpretative primacy over the others. But the acutest modern difficulty lies elsewhere, namely with how the remarkably exalted quality of the whole of biblical ecclesiology is to be interpreted in relation to the mundane reality of the actual Churches. The referent of these statements, after all, is not unknown to us from the letters of St Paul. Here it emerges unmistakably that the life of the Churches was not in every respect an edifying spectacle. Their members were capable of the grossest immorality and had a penchant for bitter factiousness. Even the most established leaders could be capable of being challenged and resisted. And we have no idea who presided at their Eucharists, which were, in any case, capable, in Paul's withering phrase, of tending to do more harm than good (1 Corinthians 11:17–22). There is a major problem here which has been ignored for too long.

Two interpretative manoeuvres prove inadequate. The first is to ignore the historical context of biblical ecclesiology as irrelevant, and to concentrate solely on the doctrine. That course is forbidden to us, because it denies the essential historicality of ecclesiology as such, namely the fundamentally narrative character of God's dealings with humankind. The great affirmations concerning the body of Christ are connected to the accounts of the actual behaviour of the Church within the category of sign. It is the same Church capable of disorder which also points to the unity of Christ's body. To extract the edifying doctrine from the mundane (but not merely mundane) reality is to create an abstract and idealized impression of the Church. In this way it becomes all too easy to legitimate the modern structures of the Church and covertly to ignore the fact that they, too, similarly participate in the ambiguities of history.

The second manoeuvre is to insulate the New Testament period from subsequent history, and fail to see the faith communities as undergoing developments of which the documents only contain adumbrations. It has been realized for a considerable time that the New Testament provides evidence for the way in which the Churches grow as institutions and resolve their problems (the 'routinization of charisma' discussion). Of course, it is correct to say that one may not simply make of a sociological process a normative statement. The fact that the Pastoral Epistles have already turned charismatic leaders into ordained officials, if that is what they have done, does not imply of itself that the development was inevitable, still less a process guided by the Holy Spirit. But it is impossible to ignore the fact that during the New Testament period developments in the life of the Church were under way which had come to no final conclusion by the end of the first century, and which went on working themselves through as the Church grew in size, influence and complexity. All this means that solutions which might have been available to one Church community in the 60s and 70s of the first century were not available to the Church of the second and third centuries, still less to the modern Western European Churches. Inevitably we are committed to an effort of theological imagination to project the trajectory of the biblical Churches into the modern world.

Orthodox, Roman Catholics and Anglicans have understood this very well, but have offered characteristically different solutions. The Orthodox require a holistic doctrine of tradition, of which the ancient sees are the embodiment. Roman Catholics allow tradition to develop to the point where it has evolved a final question-deciding authority. The classic Anglican solution involved what has been called quinquesecularism, the doctrine that the unanimous consent of the first five centuries contain all that the Churches need to know about the faith, with neither deviation nor accretion. If none of these is any longer credible in its strictest form, I should want to affirm the Catholic instinct without hesitation on the ground of the historicality of the Church. That is to say, to be God's Church on earth is to be his sign in the midst of ambiguous and changing circumstances. Yet Anglicans are right to insist that we should under no circumstances lose contact with the biblical witness to the Church in its full historic reality. Processes in the Church cannot be turned into the equivalent of revelation. Although the Church requires a decision-making process, all the relevant criteria in matters relating to salvation are open to all believers because they are biblical. The biblical portrait of the Church, warts and all, remains foundational in the capacity to inform the minds of those who continue to discern the Church's way in new circumstances.

Baptismal ecclesiology

To complete this paper, which is a most incomplete orientation on the doctrine of the Church, I wish to deal with one central topic on which Anglicans have, I believe, an instinct but not yet, or not adequately, a theology. It concerns the fate of the theology of baptism in the context of widespread agreement between the Orthodox and Roman Catholics on what is called 'Eucharistic ecclesiology'. Associated with the work of Fr Nicholas Afanasiev, and strongly developed in altered form by John Zizioulas, Eucharistic ecclesiology is specifically mentioned in the Congregation for the Doctrine of the Faith's recent docu-

ment. Here the Letter is at some pains to distance itself
from one of the implications of a form of Eucharistic
ecclesiology, namely that it validates the assembly of the
local Church 'in such a way as to render any other principle of unity or universality inessential' (para. 11). On the
contrary, the document argues

> the oneness and indivisibility of the Eucharistic body of the
> Lord implies the oneness of his mystical body, which is the one
> and indivisible Church. From the Eucharistic centre arises the
> necessary openness of every celebrating community, of every
> particular Church. By allowing itself to be drawn into the open
> arms of the Lord, it achieves insertion into his one and undiv-
> ided body. For this reason too the existence of the Petrine minis-
> try, which is a foundation of the unity of the episcopate and of
> the universal Church, bears a profound correspondence to the
> Eucharistic character of the Church.

But even subject to this caveat, the root and centre of
ecclesial communion is said to exist in the Holy Eucharist
(para. 5), because the Eucharistic sacrifice 'receives the
entire gift of salvation' (para. 11).

But what then of baptism? Since the Decree on Ecumenism of Vatican II, a Roman Catholic theology has been
committed to a strong affirmation that 'baptism . . . constitutes the sacramental bond of unity existing among all
who through it are reborn' (*Unitatis Redintegratio*, para. 22).
But the question immediately arises whether one could be
'truly incorporated into the crucified and glorified Christ
and . . . reborn to a sharing of the divine life' without
also being a member of Christ's One, Holy, Catholic, and
Apostolic Church? It is difficult to imagine how incorporation of the kind asserted could be distinguished from
such 'membership', biblically conceived as being a limb or
organ of Christ. In this case, a concept of 'Church' must
exist to which baptised members of non-Roman Churches
properly belong.

In this connection one may argue that Roman Catholic
theology does not permit one to say, as has recently been
suggested, that the decision to ordain women to the priest-

hood implies that the Church of England no longer belongs to the One, Holy, Catholic, and Apostolic Church. What Roman Catholic theology in fact asserts is that through faith and baptism every member of the faithful is 'inserted into the One, Holy, Catholic, and Apostolic Church' ('The Church as Communion', para. 10), and that this is an 'introduction' into 'ecclesial communion', involving 'a certain communion albeit imperfect' with Roman Catholic Christians. Again, one must say that the only form of 'communion', theologically conceived as the consequence of baptism, is communion *within* the body of Christ.

Of course, the same passage on the ecumenical importance of baptism immediately qualifies this affirmation with a strong reservation.

> Baptism, of itself, is only a beginning, a point of departure, for it is wholly directed towards the acquiring of fullness of life in Christ. Baptism is thus ordained towards a complete profession of faith, a complete incorporation into the system of salvation such as Christ himself willed it to be, and finally towards a complete integration into Eucharistic communion. (*Unitatis Redintegratio*, para. 22)

This raises several points of importance. First, one must agree that baptism is the point of entry into a life which involves growing into the full stature of Christ. That life may be stultified through various obstacles and impediments, among which may be a failure to make use of the available means of grace, especially the Eucharistic sacrament. Baptism properly understood thus signifies a process of growth. I find this point nowhere better put than in the Public Baptism of Infants of the Book of Common Prayer, where the priest, after the baptism, exhorts the godfathers and godmothers in the following terms:

> Remembering always that Baptism doth represent unto us our profession; which is to follow the example of our Saviour Christ, and to be made like unto him; that as he died, and rose again

41

for us, so should we, who are baptised, die from sin, and rise again unto righteousness; continually mortifying all our evil and corrupt affections, and daily proceeding in all virtue and godliness of living.

In a certain sense it improperly diminishes baptism to speak of it as 'only a beginning'. Baptism represents the totality of the Christian life, and we live our way into it assisted by all the available means of grace. Again, in a certain sense it is misleading to speak of a further 'complete incorporation into a system of salvation' beyond baptism. One should rather reserve the word 'incorporation' for the baptismal event itself. Theologically, it would not be tolerable to hold that baptism is a partial incorporation into Christ, as if those who were 'only' baptised were incomplete in their membership of Christ. But, of course, complete incorporation into Christ in baptism is compatible with a growing realization of the ramifications of that incorporation, and enjoyment of its consequences. Baptism, therefore, essentially belongs to the realm of sign, signifying a not fully realised communion with the risen Christ, a communion of which we have a foretaste, but not the whole, within human history and experience.

At the same time the Roman Catholic theological tradition is entirely justified on biblical grounds in asserting the unity of the sacraments of baptism and Eucharist. There are no first-century analogies for our modern situation in which Churches recognize one another's baptisms, but not their Eucharists. The growing normativity of infant baptism and the problem of the Donatist schism led to a separation of baptism from Eucharistic communion which has plagued Western church life and theology from the days of Augustine. The choice is apparently to emphasize either Eucharistic fellowship and correspondingly to diminish baptismal communion; or vice versa. The Roman Catholic tradition has consistently followed the former course, and speaks of 'wounds' of varying degrees of seriousness in those Churches which fail to acknowledge that communion with the Pope is one of the constituents internal to the life of communion in Christ's body, the Church. It is important to realize that Anglicans have never held this view, and that their instinctive ecclesiology gives a rather different account of the relation of baptism and Eucharist within the body of Christ. Anglicans hold, with the whole scriptural and early patristic witness, that initiation (a term here consciously preferred to baptism, and in explicit acknowledgement of the problematic relationship of baptism and confirmation) is initiation into the Eucharistic community. On this basis, for example, canonical permission to partake of the Holy Communion is given to 'baptised persons who are communicant members of other Churches which subscribe to the doctrine of the Holy Trinity, and who are in good standing in their own Church' (Canon B15A(1)(b)).

The discrimination implied in the phrase 'which subscribe to the doctrine of the Holy Trinity' is directly related to baptism in the name of the Holy Trinity, and confirms the fact that judgement is required about the authenticity of the faith-community from which the potential communicant derives.

Consistent with this is the long, consistent and distinguished tradition in the Church of England which insists that other Churches, including Trinitarian non-episcopal Churches, really participate in the One, Holy, Catholic, and Apostolic Church of Christ. That affirmation, made in the light of a common baptism, is compatible with a judgement that different Churches may be in various states of error, of varying degrees of seriousness, in relation to particular doctrines. The 'branch theory', first put forward in the nineteenth century, is a radical and highly disputable curtailment of that understanding, with a view to limiting 'the Catholic Church' to three 'branches', Eastern, Roman, and Anglican. It has been soundly criticized by numerous Anglicans, among them H. B. Swete and A. M. Ramsey, and has no title to be regarded as more than one privately advanced theological proposal within an Anglican spectrum. A more consistent judgement, and at the same time a more authoritative one, is contained in the Meissen

43

Declaration in which the Church of England solemnly acknowledges the Churches of the Federation of the Evangelical Churches in the German Democratic Republic and of the Evangelical Church in Germany to be Churches 'belonging to the One, Holy, Catholic, and Apostolic Church of Jesus Christ, and truly participating in the apostolic mission of the whole people of God'.

In reflecting on these and similar judgements it appears that Anglican ecclesiology has been more deeply influenced by one of its Thirty-nine Articles than it is, perhaps, consciously aware. Article 19 on the Church is a curiously one-sided statement about the visible church, from which, as Professor Oliver O'Donovan has pertinently observed, the invisible church has disappeared. It then passes to what at first sight appears a discouragingly negative verdict on the Churches of Jerusalem, Alexandria, Antioch, and Rome. These, we are assured, have erred, not merely in living and ceremonies, but also in matters of faith. This proposition has the liberating consequence of denying the existence of error-free zones, and through it Anglicans have acquired a certain instinct for critical self-appraisal. As O'Donovan appositely comments:

> Every 'particular' Church that has ever existed or does exist has erred. It is for this reason that we must remain humble about our institutions and resist the temptation to identify this or that one with the Catholic Church. (*On the 39 Articles*, p. 95)

The reformability of each particular Church must patently include its ability to correct its own mistakes at reformation.

The tragic failure of the Churches to realize the intrinsic connection between baptism and Eucharist also involves Anglicans who are inextricably implicated in the consequences. But in this case there exists no motive to deny the full affirmation of the efficacy of Christian baptism on profession of Trinitarian faith as bestowing membership in the body of Christ. This, as we have seen in the case of the Gospel of St John, establishes the boundary between Church and world, the passage from darkness to life and bondage to freedom. In terms of its significatory character the sacrament is both instrument and sign, both effecting radical change and pointing to more than is yet visibly realized. Nothing in the Churches' failure to keep Eucharistic communion in harmony with the baptismal beginning should encourage Anglicans to diminish the life-altering character of the sacrament of baptism.

At the same time, the Anglican has no obligation to minimize the intrinsic connection which exists between the unity of Christ's body, the Eucharistic sacrament, and the agent or enabler of Eucharistic celebration, the bishop. Eucharistic ecclesiology, shorn of certain exaggerated nuances, still has a powerful message. Precisely because it is a repeated sacrament, the eucharist actualizes again and again the completed reality of the reconciliation of God and humankind in the Cross. The Eucharistic sacrifice is, as such, theologically inseparable from the baptismal sacrifice. It belongs intrinsically to the institutional reality of the Church to order baptism and Eucharist in such a way that this connection is constantly made clear. From this arises the task of the episcopate, to ordain by prayer and the laying on of hands those whose principal task it is to baptise and celebrate Eucharist publicly with, for, and in the face of the whole Church.

It follows that those who perceive this connection are necessarily committed to the restoration of the visible unity of the Church. To defend this connection I take to be the ground of, and principle reason for, Anglican intransigence on the subject of the episcopate. At the same time such arguments do not entail the theories of defects or wounds in non-episcopal Churches, compensated for by mysterious toppings-up of uncovenanted mercies to account for the obvious signs of grace and holiness which they display. In terms of sacramental theology, the reality of baptism sufficiently accounts for the gracious presence and unstinting activity of the Holy Spirit in each of the Churches; and the mundane and ordinary failures of the historic institutions include their failure to agree about ordained ministry and the Eucharist, and so to preserve the unity established in the baptismal sacrifice. Despite this the Eucharistic sacrament continues to be a sign and foretaste of the realization of greater unity in the eschatological banquet; and in the episcopal Churches the structural unity of the episcopate, even in the unreconciled form of parallel jurisdiction, contains the promise of a future unity, including the potential of a universal primacy.

It is not for the sake of yet more argument about the sex of the priesthood that I have produced this paper. But there will be those who will want to know what conclusions might be drawn from such an ecclesiology in the context of our present situation. We have now to assume that Anglicans are, as a matter of fact, defining or redefining themselves ecclesiologically in every part of the world. It is, despite what its detractors say, not a negligible occurrence, and the rest of the world Church treats it as considerable. For me, something happened when the suffragan bishop of Namibia, speaking with the authenticity of the suffering Church of Southern Africa, told me that he wanted his province to be the kind of place where those who were opposed to this development could feel they belonged and were honoured alongside those in favour. The Anglican communion has plainly embarked on a vocation to which it is impossible to predict the end, and it has done so believing that it has acted in obedience to its Lord. Though opponents deny it, the actions are claimed to be totally consistent with continuing to transmit the essential priesthood and episcopate of the Catholic Church. In these orders priests and bishops, if women, will continue to intend to do what Christ has delivered to his Church to perform in the sacraments of baptism and Eucharist. The consequence that some Anglicans will not be able conscientiously to recognize these sacramental actions is seen as less damaging than disobedience to a vision of an inclusive ministry.

From the ecclesiology I have sketched I wish to draw one seriously critical and one positive comment. The critical remark concerns the damage done to the visible unity of the Church. The Roman Catholic Church's official pronouncements have been consistent in their warnings, and they have every right to their expressions of profound regret at a new and grave obstacle to reconciliation. Of course, it might be said that very little encouragement has recently been given by the Vatican to Anglican-Roman Catholic relations; or that there is absolutely no sign of change in relation to the Papal pronouncement against Anglican orders as such. But the context of ecclesiastical diplomacy is not a self-sufficient world, and no Anglican has any right to do other than view with genuine dismay the widening gulf which separates us after explicit and repeated warnings. The ecclesiology I have sketched requires Anglicans to take the unity of the Church with the greatest seriousness and to see the ordained ministry as its enabler. It is inconceivable that this unity should be harmed without grave cause, or in a mood of absent-minded or light-hearted modishness. It will not do, therefore, to defend the development as anything other than an act of eschatological obedience to the future of the Catholic Church, a temporary act from one part of the Church in the cause of a greater and deeper eventual unity of the whole.

The second, positive, comment I make in negative form. It could always be, on sound Anglican principles, that the Anglican Churches are in error. There is here something of a doctrinal crux for those who oppose this development. Either, it appears, they must reach the conclusion that so seriously is the Anglican communion in error that it is evidence for the truth of another Church claiming immunity from errors of such gravity; or they must find a way of believing the teaching of a Church for whom the possibility of at least temporary error is part of its doctrinal stance. I have already defended the truth of the Article on error in the Church on the grounds that it permits Anglicans to be consistently self-critical, even of the Church's reformations. The essential point is the vulnerability of the truth, and it is this which makes self-congratulatory posturing wholly inappropriate. If we are open to his truth, God will not deny us his grace, especially not at his

47

Eucharist. On that condition alone, I am prepared for my
Church to be in error until such time as God vouchsafes
it a new vision.

3 The Content of the Catholic Faith*

Jeffrey John

In 1947 Dorothy L. Sayers wrote an essay called *The Dogma is the Drama*[1] on the relevance of Christian doctrine to real life. In it she drew up a kind of question-and-answer catechism, supplying the answers from the general ideas which she felt the ordinary person has about the content of Christian teaching. It goes like this.

Question What does the Church think of God the Father?

Answer He is omnipotent and holy. He created the world and imposed on man conditions impossible of fulfilment. He is very angry if these are not carried out. He sometimes interferes by means of arbitrary judgment and miracles, distributed with a good deal of favouritism. He likes to be truckled to, and is always ready to pounce on anybody who trips up over a difficulty in the Law, or is having a bit of fun. He is rather like a dictator, only larger and more arbitrary.

Question What does the Church think of God the Son?

Answer He is in some way to be identified with Jesus of Nazareth. It was not his fault that the world was made like this and, unlike God the Father, he is friendly to man and did his best to reconcile man and God. He has a good deal of influence with God, and if you want anything done, it's best to apply to him.

Question What does the Church think of God the Holy Ghost?

*© Jeffrey John 1993

Answer I don't know exactly. He was never seen or heard of till Whit Sunday. There is a sin against him which damns you for ever, but nobody knows what it is.

Question What is the doctrine of the Holy Trinity?

Answer 'The Father incomprehensible, the Son incomprehensible, the Holy Ghost incomprehensible' – the whole thing incomprehensible. Something put in by theologians to make it more difficult. Nothing to do with daily life or reality.

Question What was Jesus Christ like in real life?

Answer He was a good man – so good as to be called the Son of God. He was meek and mild and preached a simple religion of love and pacifism. He had no sense of humour. If we try to live like him, God the Father will let us off being damned hereafter and only have us tortured in this life instead.

Question What is meant by the Atonement?

Answer God wanted to damn everybody, but his vindictive sadism was sated by the crucifixion of his own Son, who was quite innocent, and therefore a particularly attractive victim. God now only damns people who don't follow Christ or who never heard of him.

Question What does the Church think of sex?

Answer God made it necessary to the machinery of the world, and tolerates it, provided the parties (a) are married, and (b) get no pleasure out of it.

Question What does the Church call sin?

Answer Sex (otherwise than as excepted above); getting drunk; saying 'damn'; murder, and cruelty to dumb animals; not going to church; most kinds of amusement. 'Original sin' means that anything we enjoy doing is wrong.

Question What is faith?

Answer Resolutely shutting your eyes to scientific fact.

Question What is the human intellect?

Answer   A barrier to faith.

Question   What are the seven Christian virtues?

Answer   Respectability; childishness; mental timidity; dullness; sentimentality; censoriousness, and depression of spirits.

Question   Wilt thou be baptised in this faith?

Answer   NO FEAR!

If this strikes a chord, I fear it is because Dorothy Sayers' caricature is as uncomfortably close to reality now as it was then. How much further have we come since the 1940s in communicating a sensible Christian faith? Most of the misunderstandings in those answers are still widespread, and still hold back many people of intelligence and goodwill from supposing that the Church says anything believable. It has been my observation in both colleges and parishes that often the first step in teaching and evangelism has to be exploding some caricature impression of Christianity which has been picked up along the way, and making it clear that faith does not mean lobotomizing either your conscience or your common sense.

My own Anglo-Catholicism, like Dorothy Sayers', was conditioned by revolt against various caricatures: first the fundamentalism I was fed as a child; then the 'Christian Union' version of the same which so afflicts student life in this country; then other, blander caricatures which seemed stronger on intellect, and stronger still on establishment respectability, but woefully lacking in faith and fire. Rejecting these, I embraced a full-blooded Anglican Catholicism, because it seemed to me then, as it seems to me now, the only version of Christianity that I could believe with passion and gusto – but without leaving brains or humanity behind.

I still believe it. For all the backbiting and hurt there has been in recent years, I cannot define myself or Affirming Catholicism against the Anglo-Catholicism that converted me and brought me to Christ. Of course, I could weep for the ways in which it too has become a caricature; but I can only see this movement as part of it, however unwelcome a part. I hope we shall not stop trying to convince the whole Catholic movement in the Anglican Church that, contrary to current fears, our place and calling have not changed, and that our hang-ups about women priests and authority and Rome are precisely that: hang-ups, failures of self-respect and self-understanding that should have been cleared away long ago. I shall have to defend this view later. But I insist: it remains our duty to challenge the caricatures with a warm Catholic faith in its fullness, and to make that faith intelligible and attractive to others, inside the Church and out.

It seems ambitious to the point of foolishness, but the purpose of this talk is to outline the content of such a faith. It is not an alternative catechism to Dorothy Sayers', though I hope it may help answer some of the questions she raised. It is structured around the Apostles' Creed, but it is not a systematic commentary – far from it. It is unashamedly selective and subjective, concentrating on what seems to me to need saying now, and neglecting what seems obvious and uncontroversial.

I believe in God

You might think that this is obvious and uncontroversial, but it is not. There is a lively movement in the Church at the moment which is preaching a Christianity without God. Like other unhappy things it comes from Cambridge, mostly in the books of Don Cupitt, and it has taken its name from one of these, *The Sea of Faith*. Hugh Dawes and Anthony Freeman have recently written books in a similar vein. What they have in common is that they all dispense with a real God. God is a psychological projection of our own spiritual needs and experiences, or a metaphor for our deepest personal and social values. Prayer is a means of integrating those experiences and asserting those values – by reciting them to yourself or in groups. There is no resurrection, no afterlife, no transcendent meaning or purpose in creation or human experience.

The possible attraction of Cupitt, Dawes, and Freeman for some of us is that they start from perceiving what we and Dorothy Sayers perceive. They see that ultimately all religious language is metaphor and story; and where the metaphor or story no longer fits the insights of new knowledge and experience, they are quick to show its tragic irrelevance or downright silliness. So there are certainly passages in their books which come as a blast of fresh air, and which may carry us along cheering. It is always fun to tell the truth and knock the nonsense down. The difference is what we do next. Intelligent Catholics have always understood that of course we can never apprehend God *as he is*. In that sense it is true that all we say of him is metaphor. For that reason, as we emphasized at our last conference, Catholic tradition is constantly changing and adapting to new insights and finding new expressions; what makes it *Catholic* tradition is that it should change and adapt compatibly with its past, and with regard to the integrity of the whole. What we have to do as Catholics is the careful hard work of constantly re-evaluating and re-expressing doctrine, changing the metaphors and adapting the stories, realizing they are always inadequate to the reality they try to convey. What Cupitt, Dawes, and Freeman have done is take a quantum leap of unfaith to conclude that there never was any reality to convey anyway. For them the metaphors are *mere* metaphors, with no referent beyond ourselves. The baby and the bathwater are one.

At bottom they are good, old-fashioned, empirical atheists; the novelty is that they want to practice atheism *within* the language and liturgy of the Church. I confess I find that incomprehensible. I do not mean I want to hound them out. I don't; though I can't help feeling that if all they want is to express and promote human and social values, a poetry group or the Labour Party might do it more effectively than the Church of England.

Members of the Sea of Faith movement describe themselves as liberal Christians. This worries me because until now I have felt bound to defend the word 'liberal' against

53

the charge that it simply means unbelief. I have preferred to think it meant 'generous, enquiring, open-minded'. For that reason I was not particularly insulted when the Archdeacon of York last year called Affirming Catholics 'liberals in vestments'. But if liberal really does mean now what the *Sea of Faith* writers mean, the next time George calls us that I think we should sue.

This is why, absurd as it seems, it needs saying clearly that we really believe in a real and personal God; and as our baptismal promises make clear, *Credo in unum deum* means we believe *and trust* in him. We not only assent to his existence, we commit ourselves in relationship to him. In the most profound sense, it is our relationship with him which *is* our faith, and everything else in the Creed flows from it. Without him there is nothing worth having.

I believe in God the Father

We all rush to say that this does not mean that God is literally a bloke, but is that enough? Many of us, including me, still have to take fully on board the fact that the overwhelming patriarchy of Christian language is felt as an oppression by many women. We ought to welcome the rediscovery of perfectly orthodox female imagery for God, so that we can quite properly call her Mother as well as Father, or Parent or Sustainer. If all humanity is made in God's image, it matters that the female aspect of God is given full weight, it matters that both sexes of humanity should be represented in the priesthood, and it matters that the language of the liturgy should not reflect the dominance or exclusion of one sex by the other.

Of course, there are limits. We are bounded by the particularity of the Incarnation. When an American Anglican dean some years ago erected a crucifix with a female figure in his cathedral, the offence was not only against taste but against the historicity of the faith. We are bounded, too, by doctrines of creation and revelation. Attempts to bypass them and create a synthesis of feminist Christianity with 'new age' Gaia-worship and the like are, to say the least, misguided. The danger of aberrations like these are that they give easy propaganda to those who would prefer the whole issue of women and the Church to go away. We must not allow that to happen. At our last conference we were pretty mealy-mouthed about women priests. I hope there are no reservations now, and that we are ready to welcome and weigh the new insights they will bring. Catholic Christianity in general is so tainted and weakened by the degradation of women; Affirming Catholicism, in however small a way, must be trying to put that right.

It is undeniable that a major impetus behind this movement has been Anglo-Catholicism's pathetic inability to face its current problems with sex and gender, particularly women priests and homosexuality. I do not propose to discuss these subjects: if you want to pursue them, let me refer you to two excellent green booklets in the Affirming Catholicism series.[2] The fact that we have tried to face these issues constructively has meant that we have been dismissed in some quarters as a two-issue affair, 'the movement for women at the altar and men in bed', to quote one unreconstructed wit. That is to be expected. What counts, once again, is that we do the careful hard work of showing *why* affirming women priests or *why* affirming decent, Christian same-sex relationships is not part of a 'secular liberal agenda', still less of a doctrine that 'anything goes', but a necessary development of Catholic tradition itself, called forth by new knowledge, a new social situation, and a new sense of justice. Nor is it only a matter of teaching. These are fear-ridden issues, often complicated by hidden psychological motives. As much as by teaching, fears need to be allayed by example – whether by making visible the example of faithful, Catholic women priests, or of faithful, Catholic gay couples. Theologically, the battle on these issues is won. What we have to keep combating is the prejudice, invincible ignorance, and ingrained hypocrisy of centuries.

Almighty, Maker of heaven and earth

Ever since the Copernican Revolution science and faith in God as Creator have seemed to be moving apart. Yet now it seems seriously possible that they are starting to reconverge. Advanced physics has passed so far beyond a Newtonian idea of the universe that it seems to speak once again in metaphysical terms, and, what is more, often in terms which virtually presuppose a creative purpose to the universe. Cosmologists, whether theists or not, cheerfully discuss what they call the 'anthropic principle', which refers to the observation that so far from being random or purely mechanistic, the universe seems to be mysteriously geared towards producing conscious life, value awareness, self-knowledge and direction – in short, human personhood. As the American physicist Freeman Dyson rather spookily put it, 'The Universe always knew we were coming.' God, of course, fits this very nicely, both as the transcendent generator of the process, and as the immanent personal power who calls the whole on towards his own kind of being. If I have understood correctly, it sounds remarkably like the evolutionary universe Teilhard de Chardin was speculating on forty years ago. Only now it is coming from scientists themselves.

This is a very exciting area, which Angela Tilby will open up to us later, but however compatible the new cosmology is with faith, in the end, like all science, it can only answer the question 'how?', while only faith itself can answer the question 'why?' It would be as unwise to tie God to a particular cosmology as it is to tie him to a literal belief in Genesis. In cosmology, as in theology, the story is always being refined; but God is always beyond the story. With regard to the biblical story itself, even today it still needs saying again and again that it was never intended as a historical or scientific account. It was and is a statement of faith: faith that the beginning of everything was not simply chance or arbitrariness or blind energy, but a good and personal God whose creation reflects his goodness; and that human personhood is the goal of that creation, and has a particular responsibility for it. And that statement of faith, with or without the 'anthropic principle', is no less plausible today than when Genesis was written down.

Jesus Christ his only son our Lord, conceived by the Holy Spirit, born of the Virgin Mary

Contrary to popular supposition, the main problem of the Virgin Birth (or more precisely, the Virginal Conception) of Jesus is not so much a problem about the miraculous in general as a problem about the nature of the documents that relate this particular miracle. Only Matthew and Luke tell us about the Virgin Birth, and it is perfectly clear that their birth stories are written in a non-historical genre. The two stories disagree in fundamentals anyway, so they cannot both be historically factual, and almost certainly neither is. Matthew and Luke were writing theological legends in a standard Jewish category of religious writing called *haggadah*, in order to show that Jesus fulfilled certain texts and expectations about the Messiah. One of those texts was the Messianic passage in Isaiah 7, where the Hebrew of verse 14 reads, 'a woman shall conceive and bear a son'. But in the Greek text of the Old Testament, the version which Matthew and Luke were using, the word 'young woman' had been translated as 'virgin' – and so it seems, ironically, that it was in order to fit this ambiguously translated Greek text that the idea of a virgin-born Messiah arose.

This observation, which is old hat to anyone who has done any serious New Testament theology, makes it very difficult to see the virginal conception as historical or biological fact. Like the author of Genesis, the authors of the birth narratives were not thinking or writing in those terms. However, it is crucial to underline that the literal historicity of the Virgin Birth does not affect the doctrine of the Incarnation or the uniqueness of Christ. St Paul and St John both present Christ as the Son of God, and as God's eternal Wisdom and Word made flesh, but without

57

relating their teaching to a Virgin Birth. St John, I believe, knew the story, and he also reports the Pharisees' alternative story that Jesus was illegitimate (8: 41); but he comments on neither and evidently regards both accounts of Jesus' earthly origin as equally irrelevant. What matters for him is that Christ comes ἐκ τῶν ἄνω, from above, and that he, like the believer, was born 'not of the will of man, nor of the will of flesh, but of God' (1: 18), a verse which apparently alludes to the Virgin Birth, but seems deliberately to bypass it to say that what is important is not a physical miracle, but God's initiative.

This is why, although this line of the Creed must be regarded as doubtful biological history, there is no problem in affirming what it intends to affirm – which is, that Jesus was uniquely born by God's will and act, and that by his birth God himself took the step to bridge the gap of our estrangement from him. It affirms that Jesus in his own person made incarnate the 'word' and 'wisdom' of God, meaning that all that relates God to human life – all the elements of personhood which God in his own nature has in common with those whom he made in his image – were perfectly shown forth in him. It means that Jesus' union with the Father was uniquely unbroken from the beginning. Throughout his earthly existence he was, if you like, God played in the human key.

This way of putting it seems to me to be both orthodox and intelligible to a contemporary person. Like David Jenkins, I believe we have to free the doctrine of the Incarnation, which is perfectly accessible and is central, from compulsory belief in a literal Virgin Birth, which is inaccessible and peripheral. Furthermore, as has been pointed out many times, overemphasis on a literal Virgin Birth has produced two unhappy tendencies. In the first place it has contributed to the view that sex, especially for women, is sinful, or even that it is the means of transmitting original sin. Secondly, it inevitably tends to the Docetic view that Christ, since he had no natural father, was not truly human but only God dressed up. Both those heresies have afflicted Catholicism for centuries, and since 1854 they have been reinforced in Roman Catholicism by the dogma of Mary's own Immaculate Conception and sinlessness.

What about Mary? You may think I have been very rude about her, but even if the Pharisees' story of Jesus' birth were true, it should in no way diminish our devotion to her: perhaps rather the opposite. It would be very much in keeping with the Gospels' portrayal of her as the symbol of the humble poor, whose vocation was to share in the suffering and humiliation of her Son, so that she might share in his glory. If only we can get past our obsession with her virginity, we might see her more clearly for what she is: Mary of the Magnificat, the Mother of the Dispossessed and the Disreputable, the humble and meek exalted by the one who puts down the mighty from their thrones. I want to say more about fellowship with the saints later, but Affirming Catholicism won't be any kind of Catholicism without Mary, so let us ask for her help. Let us rescue her from sickly pieties and from being a party badge, and make her a real friend, a real Mother. Let us recapture the Mariology of a marvellous mystery play I saw recently. At the end Our Lady was assumed into heaven from her kitchen, a truculent Yorkshirewoman with curlers and a plastic handbag, suddenly bathed in golden light and embraced by her Son in glory. 'Eeh, that's my lad that is!' she said. 'And don't he look gradely!'

He suffered under Pontius Pilate, was crucified, died, and was buried

One of the things that held me back longest from Christian faith was the doctrine of the atonement which I was taught as a child, and which resembled very closely the one described by Dorothy Sayers. This presented me with a picture of a Father God who was very angry with us for our sins, and who as a matter of justice had condemned us all to death. But then he sent Jesus his Son to suffer and die for us instead, and because Jesus was sinless God substituted his punishment for the one due to us. Jesus took the rap, and we got let off provided we said we believed in him.

Even at the age of ten I saw that for what it is: a logically incoherent and morally repulsive story which gives God a character that in any human being we would call pathologically criminal. Yet it is the account of the Cross which I have continued to hear in a hundred different missions and evangelistic meetings and Bible-study groups. For many Christians, 'evangelism' seems to mean working up an intolerable sense of guilt, bringing the victims to a point of emotional breakdown, then proffering this story as the means of escape, so that it is clutched and internalized and for ever after lodges this monstrous picture of God in the brain. This, God help us, is called 'being saved'. (Happily it does not always work. Some time ago I attended a student talk by two hapless missionaries who had been trying to sell this kind of thing to a remote tribe in Indonesia. They failed miserably. Not only did the tribe refuse to wear any clothes – not even the consignment of Marks and Spencer underwear the missionaries had thoughtfully taken for them – their language did not even possess a word for shame. As the lady missionary exclaimed, 'Gosh, it was dreadful. We couldn't make them feel guilty about *anything*!')

One way to understand the Cross is to see it as the ultimate point of the Incarnation. To speak of Christ's sacrifice is not to imply that there is a gulf between a nice Jesus and a nasty Father-God. Rather, as Paul puts it, 'God was in Christ reconciling us to himself.' As perfect self-sacrificing Love, God did what Love does, he put himself in the place of the beloved. God became man in Christ to identify himself with us, to put himself where we are. The Cross is the ultimate point of that self-identification. Paradoxical as it is, the bottom line of the atonement is expressed in Jesus' words, 'My God, my God, why have you forsaken me?' If we can speak like Paul of God's self-emptying in the Incarnation, then here is the point at which he empties himself completely, he shares completely even in our lostness, our alienation from him. He comes to be where we are, so that we might be where he is.

This is an understanding of the atonement which seems to me rational, humane, and also very powerful, because it means that wherever we are, God is there too, even in suffering, even in death, even in our apparent estrangement from him. Of course, I do not mean to suggest that it exhausts the whole meaning of the atonement. Much more needs to be said about the imagery of Christ's sacrifice, how it fulfils the sacrificial system of the Old Covenant, and how we should translate it into contemporary terms of self-giving and self-transcendence. Much more needs to be said about the mystery of the Passion, and how (quite apart from morbid guilt) we properly discover the weight of our own sin, and how we see responsibility for Christ's death in our own lies, betrayals, denials, and expedient compromises with injustice. Much more needs to be said about how the atonement becomes part of us; how the Cross is one instance in time of the eternal self-giving of Father and Son to one another in Trinity, and how that self-giving is made present and real for us now especially in the Mass, so that we are drawn into it, and become part of it ourselves. These are the Catholic truths of the atonement; but alas, it is the caricature account that is generally heard.

He descended into hell

The Alternative Service Book says, 'he descended to the dead', which is better, because the original says *descendit ad inferos*', which really means the 'underworld'. It was Luther and Calvin who insisted on translating it as 'hell', firstly because they held a substitutionary theory of the atonement, and thought that Jesus had to taste a bit of hell on our behalf; and secondly, because they disliked the suggestion that there was any form of afterlife other than hell or heaven. It seemed to leave room for purgatory, and they were having none of *that*. In fact, this article of the Creed is a late, fourth-century addition, which probably derives from the mysterious statement in 1 Peter 3:18–20 that between his death and Resurrection Christ went and preached to the 'imprisoned spirits'. Whatever that meant in the original, it was taken by the Church to mean that those who had died before Christ, especially the patriarchs and prophets, still got their chance of sharing in the Resurrection.

So the real importance of the descent to the dead is what it says about the justice of God. God is a God of fair play; people must get their chance of choosing for him or against him. This conviction is every bit as crucial for us today. Of all the questions I have been asked by people on the brink of faith, possibly the most frequent has been, 'What happens to non-Christians when they die?' How can a good God reject people who never had a chance to hear of him, or who got the wrong message, or who simply could not conscientiously believe? The reason the question is asked so often is that so many Christians *do* go around telling people, or at least strongly implying, that unless you sign on the Christian dotted line in this life, then when you die you fry.

The Catholic faith has always left room, and must leave room, for the salvation of souls beyond this life – because not to do so is utterly incompatible with a God of justice, let alone a God of love. Indeed, it has to leave room for growth in all of us, because which of us when we die has learned love enough to be perfectly united with God? Whether it happens in time or out of time, there must be further revelation, there must be growth, there must be healing for us all. Whether we call that condition of growth 'purgatory' hardly matters (though if we do we have to detach it very clearly from any nonsense about indulgences and the calculation of days and years); but there must be an intermediate state after death, both to satisfy God's justice and to complete the work of redemption in us all.

This issue relates closely to the way we view other faiths. Christian exclusivists often quote texts like John 14: 6, where Christ says, 'No one comes to the Father but through me,' to argue that there is no salvation for non-Christians. They forget that in John's Gospel Christ speaks as the Word, 'the Light who enlightens every one who comes into the world'. The point of calling Jesus the Word in John's Gospel is to identify him as the fulfilment of all the ways in which God has been known in all times and all places and all cultures (St Paul does the same by identifying Jesus with eternal Wisdom). God has shared his own reason and wisdom with all people made in his image, so that all can know him, however partially and imperfectly. William Temple put this very well in his Commentary on John:

> All that is noble in non-Christian systems of thought, or conduct or worship is the work of Christ upon them and in them. By the Word of God – that is to say, by Jesus Christ – Isaiah and Plato and Zoroaster and Buddha and Confucius conceived and uttered such truths as they declared. There is only one divine light; and every man in his measure is enlightened by it.

So if Jesus in John's Gospel says, 'No one comes to the Father but through me,' that does not mean that nobody goes to heaven except paid-up Christians. It means that no one comes to God except by the light, however faltering, which God has put in each one of us; and it is by that light that we shall in the end be judged. The doctrine of Christ's descent to the dead leaves room for just this hope, and reassures us that God's salvation is a great deal more just and generous than some would make it seem.

On the third day he rose again; he ascended into heaven and is seated at the right hand of the Father

Like the Virgin Birth, the problem of the Resurrection is essentially a problem about the way we approach the New Testament evidence, a matter of discerning its different registers of writing and the different kinds of truth they tell us. The first thing to observe is that in the earliest account of Christ's Resurrection, in Paul, there is no mention of an empty tomb or of Jesus being raised in the body.

63

When Paul talks about appearances of the risen Christ, to himself and to many others, he could quite possibly be talking of a non-bodily appearance. Paul also says, when speaking of our own resurrection, that flesh and blood do not inherit the kingdom of God. The resurrection life, he says, will be a completely different mode of being. When he envisages his own death he speaks of leaving his body behind in order to go to be with Christ. So it is quite plausible that Paul did not think that the afterlife depended on the physical body in any way, and he might not have been dismayed by the thought of someone finding Jesus' bones. Yet at the same time he refuted those who doubted the reality of resurrection, or who were inclined to regard it as mere metaphor, with the ringing assertion that unless it is real, 'we are of all people most to be pitied'.

I admit I find this comforting on a number of counts. In the first place, Paul's evidence is not only the earliest evidence, it is factual evidence in our own register, as opposed to the Gospel evidence which is written in a genre which is half historical, half symbolic. His own eyewitness testimony in 1 Corinthians 15, with the claim that it was corroborated by more than five hundred witnesses, is unequivocal and compelling. Secondly, the fact that Paul's account allows us to conceive of a resurrection apart from this body has obvious advantages for us, because it seems so clear that we cannot possibly rise to life in the same body we leave behind. The report of the empty tomb on the other hand, and especially the pictures in John and Luke of Jesus eating fish and having fingers poked into him, simply will not square with anything we can plausibly expect for ourselves. Paul's assertion that in the resurrection life we are in a different realm of being with new, spiritual bodies, seems both more probable and infinitely preferable. In practice, it is the spiritual model of the resurrection that I suspect the great majority of us work with.

Nevertheless, it is probably not enough. The New Testament and Catholic teaching are uniformly emphatic that God redeems us body and soul. We are not Gnostics; the whole of what we are is saved. As I mentioned, when Paul speaks of his own death before the Lord comes, he talks in purely dualist terms of his spirit going to be with the Lord. But when he talks of resurrection at the Last Trump, he uses different images which imply not so much a separation of the spirit from the body as the conversion of the body into spirit. Resurrection is like the seed becoming the plant, or like the foetus being born as the child, or like the old being consumed by the new, or being clothed over by it. Here it is not straight dualism, it is transformation, 'changing these lowly bodies into copies of his glorious body'. Furthermore, Paul and other New Testament witnesses testify that in the end, in the consummation of everything, the physical creation itself which is now 'in bondage to decay' will also be taken up and included in the glory of God's children. So perhaps, although like Paul we have to be provisional dualists with regard to our own death, that is not the end of the story. The physical creation of which our bodies are part will also ultimately share in redemption. Perhaps that is the truth which the empty tomb, whether as fact or image, is meant to show.

That is surely the point of the Ascension too. It is described only by Luke, and Luke himself puts it on two different days, on Easter day in his Gospel and forty days later in the Book of Acts, so obviously he was not being too fussy about the literal history of the matter. Like the Old Testament ascensions, or like the Assumption of Our Lady, it is a pictorial way of saying that Jesus is with God in glory. But it also underlines, like the physical resurrection stories, that he has not come on a whistle-stop tour, worn flesh for a bit, and sloughed it off to go home. The Ascension affirms that the Incarnation is eternal fact. God is united with our whole humanity, body and soul; and ultimately that whole humanity, including its scars, is destined to be with him in glory.

He will come again in glory, to judge both the quick and the dead

The doctrine of Christ's second coming has a way of making people look silly. There was a sad story just a couple of years ago of Christians in the Philippines taking the roofs off their houses so that they would not bump their heads in the rapture of the second coming, then getting very wet when the rainy season came instead. Paul and other early Christians must also have felt increasingly silly when Jesus failed to come and wind things up as soon as they thought. Failed apocalyptic expectation has been a feature of Judaism and Christianity right down to the horror of Waco, and it will be a service on the part of Catholics to point this out. Yet, even from an unbelieving point of view, it is clear that the winding-up will come. Life on earth will end, if only when the sun burns out; though it looks far more likely that we shall accomplish it first. As for the universe, who can say? Will it expand infinitely, or contract and collapse in a big black hole? We are given no dates and times, and it is sheer silliness to look for them in scripture, but faith in Christ's coming at the end of time is a way of saying what we have affirmed already: that whatever happens will happen within God's care, and that he is both the origin and the goal of what he created in love.

To understand judgment, it helps to translate the courtroom imagery into terms of revelation, response, and relationship. When I die I expect to go to purgatory (I hope that is not overoptimistic). I expect in purgatory to be faced with a clearer revelation of the love of God, and in the light and fire of that love I expect to feel a kind of pain – the kind of pain we feel on earth when we are shown up for what we really are, or when we are loved by someone and we know we do not deserve to be; the kind of pain Peter felt when he said, 'Depart from me, O Lord,' because it hurt to be so transparent to the presence of holiness. If by the time I die I have learned to love properly, learned how to lose myself in love to find my real self, then the pain will be less. If I am as I am now, I expect the pain will be very great; and that will be both my judgment and my healing. But as St John says, it is a judgment that starts now, because the light is here already, and it always faces us with a choice: to approach and be seen, or to turn away. So it will not be a question of court and judge, thrones and books. It will be being what we are in the glare of what we are meant to be.

If you ask if I believe in hell – yes, I do. I believe in it because God made us free, like himself, and in this life or the next it is always open to us to turn away from the pain of light to the comforting dark. God will not consign us; but we may consign ourselves. Even in this life, how often we might prefer in our cowardice or egotism to choose nothing, non-being, rather than face the pain and sacrifice of love. What else can hell be than nothing? If we consistently and consciously turn away from the Source of our being, then we are choosing not to be. As C. S. Lewis insisted, 'God is the one without whom Christians say Nothing is strong. Nothing is holy. And Nothing is very strong, strong enough to steal away a man's soul.' Hell is not heat and light, it is cold and dark. Not something but Nothing.[3]

I believe in the Holy Spirit

I am not going to discuss whether the Spirit proceeds from the Father alone (as the Eastern Church says) or from the Father and the Son (as in the West). Mind you, some think it is crucial. At theological college I sat next to a student who always recited in the Nicene Creed,

> I believe in the Holy Ghost, the Lord the Giver of Life,
> Who proceedeth from the Father, TUM TI TUM.

More important (at least, so I have found in confirmation classes) is the question, In what sense is the Spirit a person of the Trinity? People can envisage the Father and the Son as persons, but the best that most of us manage with the Spirit is to think of a bird. It needs explaining that the word

67

person in Trinitarian doctrine does not mean person in our normal sense, but rather the way we perceive the personal reality of the one God. It helps perhaps to know that the word comes from the Latin *persona*, meaning mask or appearance. The persons of the Trinity are aspects under which we perceive the life and action of the one God.

I realize that at this point the clever clogs among you will want to shout out that this is none other than the Modalist heresy, and so it is. But we might correct it by pointing out the other literally vital truth about the Trinity, which is that God is not, as it were, one static blob that can be looked at in three days, but he exists in his own nature as active, dynamic relationship, a personal relationship of love into which we are drawn. In his own essential nature, God is already community, three persons in the complete harmony of love, such that each is wholly complete and individual, yet wholly given to the others. It is our destiny, as persons made in God's image, ultimately to be the same: to be united with the persons of God himself in Trinity. That is what heaven will be. That's what we are meant to be learning now in the Church, the foreshadowing and training ground for the divine Community. And the Holy Spirit who proceeds from God (however he proceeds) is none other than God's presence and power working in us to draw us into that unity with him and with one another, giving us a foretaste now of what shall be for ever.

If you ask if the Holy Spirit is the exclusive property of Christians, or worse still, of some subgroup of the Born Again, the answer is clearly No. The Spirit is already active in creating and sustaining all things: he is the Giver of Life in very sense, even when we are blind to his operation. But when we are not blind, when we open our hearts and minds to God in a conscious response, then we let him in in a different, more powerful way, and we can talk in a real sense of personal inspiration, vocation and gifting. We become channels of his working in us and through us, not as automata, but in the way he wants, through our own willed co-operation with his power and purpose.

I am going to skip the Church because I want to put it last.

I believe in the Communion of Saints

Most Anglicans do not have a significant belief in the Communion of Saints: we are too earth-bound and moralistic. If we think about them at all we think of them as dead heroes of the past, distant paragons of virtue that we must struggle to imitate. Yet to be honest I find it far easier and certainly more encouraging to relate to the saints in their weaknesses than in their strengths. Perhaps it is a Welsh trait. Take my favourite saint, St Pyr, the first Abbot of Caldy in West Wales, who died by getting roaring drunk and falling into the abbey well. The Celtic Church made him a saint anyway. St Pyr, patron of the pootled, pray for us! Or St James, another favourite. I love the legend of James's death, when the executioner, an apostate Christian, asked for his absolution. The hagiographer remarks that there was a very long silence while James underwent a tremendous internal struggle, until he finally pronounced the absolution – through firmly clenched teeth!

The Bible, of course, calls all of us saints, and that is the point. It is the sanctified humanity of the saints that inspires, because it relates to where we are and reminds us we are in with a chance. There is something particularly Catholic about that perception, and it is one reason why Catholicism is more fun. But what matters even more is being aware of the presence of the saints with us now. The thing that is really wrong with the standard Anglican view of saints is its awful, dead historicism. Think of all those dreary Prayer Book collects about 'striving after their righteous and godly ensamples'. We are supposed to believe in eternal life, for God's sake! The saints are not dead and gone, they are alive and here, living brothers

69

and sisters in the body of Christ – that is what communion means.

And how can you have communion without communication? Of course, we should talk to saints and ask for the help of their prayers, just as we should pray for the dead. They are the atmosphere we breathe. That is not medieval mystagogy, it simply follows from our faith that in Christ death cannot divide, we are members of one another whether we happen to be here or beyond. Our liturgy and our Churches should express that presence, the fact that we worship not alone and in a void but in company with the whole Body of Christ, 'with angels and archangels and all the company of heaven'. Making the eternal Presence real, tangible, and warm has always been the glory of Catholic liturgy. In a society that is starved of the transcendent, and in a Church where worship is so often man-centred and banal, we have little that is more precious to offer.

I believe in the forgiveness of sins

Something else that the Catholic movement has failed to commend to the whole Anglican Church, and that we even seem to have lost nerve about ourselves, is sacramental confession. Because it is difficult, going to confession has long been seen as the true mark of a Catholic in the Church of England, and frankly it is a prejudice I share. Michael Ramsey used to say that when he was a curate he only ever preached on two subjects, confession and hell – on the grounds that if you do not go to one you go to the other. A slight overstatement, perhaps, but even in later life he felt there was truth in it.

One of my hopes about the priesting of women is that, in bringing new pastoral and spiritual insights, they will bring a renewal of confessional ministry. There are so many women counsellors, women deacons and religious sisters who are excellent spiritual directors, and who have said how often in the course of their ministry they have longed to be able to give absolution. Of course, there is a lot of work to be done on confession. We still have to get over all the abuses, the Dave Allen-type caricatures of the confessional, which have made it ridiculous in the minds of many. We need to re-examine our concepts of sin, guilt, and responsibility. We have to get rid of the old mechanical, legalist view and look at the new ways of performing the sacrament, how it relates to counselling and direction, how it can form part of a process of spiritual growth which the Church is there to assist. Confession is something we must be seen to be offering, seriously and professionally, because, as any therapist or GP will tell you, there are millions of people out there burdened with guilt and self-hatred who need nothing so much as to hear those words, 'By the authority committed to me I absolve you.' To be able to say *with authority*, 'You are forgiven, you are wanted, you are loved, now go out and *live*' – that is an enormously healing thing, a priceless gift which no one else is in a position to offer. Yet at the moment it is a gift which we are mostly burying in the ground.

I have said all I want to say about the resurrection of the dead. So last of all:

I believe in the Holy Catholic Church

The catholic Church means first and foremost the Church universal, the company of all Christian people on earth and in heaven. In that most fundamental sense we are all members of the catholic Church and no baptized Christian of any denomination can be more 'catholic' than any other. Bishop Sykes has expounded this fundamental sense of the word very clearly in his paper.

But we also use the word Catholic, with a capital C, in a second, narrower sense (quite apart from its popular use as an abbreviation of 'Roman Catholic') and this sense is inescapably bound up with questions of Church tradition, structure, and authority. The New Testament shows us Christ sending out his Apostles with authority to preach, teach, heal, baptize, absolve, and exercise discipline in the Church. As the Church grew that apostolic authority had

71

to be handed on in the continuing institution. The earliest patterns of ministry were untidy, but they crystallized remarkably quickly into the ministry of bishops, priests, and deacons. From the second century onwards the structure of delegated apostolic authority through bishops was seen as a safeguard of right teaching in the Church, a means of deciding the correct interpretation of scripture and tradition, and a powerful unifying force against fragmentation and heresy. So Catholic in its second sense came to mean being united with that mainstream of tradition through an episcopal succession. At the Reformation, almost uniquely, the Anglican Church claimed to remain united with that mainstream, and so to remain Catholic in this particular sense, despite having reformed itself of what it called Roman errors, and having removed itself from Papal authority. In the last century the Tractarians and others re-emphasized that claim of Anglicanism to be a true part of Catholic Christendom in this narrower sense, and they also filled out that claim by reviving or reintroducing Catholic doctrines and practices which had been thrown out with the Reformation bathwater. That is our inheritance as Anglican Catholics (Affirming or otherwise), and it is an inheritance to defend and be hugely proud of.

It also means that being an Anglican Catholic has always meant occupying an ecclesiologically precarious position. Catholics in the Church of England have always had to accept that, as well as a mission to the world, we have a mission to our own Church. Those of us who are priests have clung resolutely to the conviction that we are not priests of a sect or a denomination, but priests of the One, Holy, Catholic, and Apostolic Church in fully the same sense of our Roman and Orthodox brethren; and we have held to that conviction regardless of what they think we are, and regardless of what half our own Church thinks too. To some this has always seemed madness; but to those of us who stand in the Catholic tradition it is fundamental.

This, of course, is the heart of the Catholic problem with women priests. Even for those who have no theological objection, the question remains, Can we do this unilaterally and still claim to preserve Catholic order? It jars on the rawest nerve of Anglo-Catholicism: *Can we still claim to be the Real Thing?* Plenty of Catholics believe it would be all right and even desirable for Anglicans to ordain women priests, provided that the Pope and the Orthodox did it as well; but can we do it on our own and still say that ours are the same as theirs are?

In a word, *Yes.* There is no qualitative difference between this move and other things that make us Anglican Catholics rather than another kind of Catholic. If the historic ministry is part of what constitutes us as a Catholic Church in the narrow sense (and I am old fashioned enough to believe it is), the inclusion of women does not inherently change it. It does not alter the role or sacramental status of bishop, priest, or deacon. It does not jeopardize the Catholic understanding of order and authority. It does not interrupt or interfere with Apostolic Succession. It does not mean sawing off one leg of the Lambeth Quadrilateral. Ecclesiologically and ecumenically it makes not a bit of difference, least of all *vis-à-vis* Rome – because we cannot gloss over the harsh fact that the Romans deny our orders anyway. *Apostolicae Curae* has been in place since 1896, and has never looked like being lifted, not even in the heady days of the Anglican/Roman Catholic International Commission and Pope John Paul's visit to Canterbury. Even if we had decided against women priests, reconciliation was not in sight. Before the vote took place, the extremely chilly Vatican response to ARCIC made that crystal clear.

Catholics in the Anglican Church have for far too long undermined their mission or simply made themselves look silly by a schizoid or slavish attitude to Rome. While we all owe some debt to Roman Catholicism, at least liturgically, there is an inherent self-contradiction in the Anglo-Papalist position which has always had a corrosive and weakening effect on the movement as a whole. Great good may come out of the present upheaval, if it is only to make Anglo-Catholics face that fact and find some self-respect as *Anglicans*.

The decision to ordain women priests is very much in

keeping with the essential nature of Anglicanism as an autonomous, pioneering part of Catholic Christendom. It is not the first issue in which Anglicans will have led and Rome followed. Now that we have done it, we have to pray the rest of the Catholic Church will sooner rather than later come round to it – and that they will come to a sane view on a few other issues too.

Let us not forget that for years now the Catholic movement in the Church of England has been in dreadful decline. It has failed to communicate or command respect, and the cutting edge of theology and evangelism has long passed elsewhere. Catholic leadership, especially in the Societies, has been negative, fundamentalist, and fearful. Now all it offers is the impossible choice of reneging on the past and submitting to Rome, or else pressing up the blind alley of 'alternative episcopal oversight' – a proposal which cuts at the roots of Catholic order far more deeply than the ordination of women, and which would doom its adherents to slow extinction in semi-apartheid from their own Church.

All this pain and mess – and for what? It needs shouting from the rooftops that the ordination of women is not a disaster for Catholics, it is a God-given chance to break out of the morass we were already in, to give up false securities and fears and open up to new life and growth. In a situation where for so long we seem to have been faced with Hobson's Choice – between Protestant or Papal fundamentalism on the one hand, or bland establishment liberalism on the other a full-faith affirming Catholicism has everything to offer, and not just to the Church of England but to the whole of the Catholic Church.

So for God's sake let us welcome women priests and get on with the Catholic agenda. We have lost none of the riches we had, and there is far more still to gain and give. As I said at the beginning, it was Anglican Catholicism that brought me to Christ, it is the best expression I know of his truth and love, and the surest means of growing up in him. This is where I want to be, and it is the faith I want to share. It has not disappeared from the Church of England. Please God, it is on the way back.

1 In *Creed or Chaos*, London, Methuen, 1947.
2 *Why Women Priests? The Ordination of Women and the Apostolic Ministry* by Jonathan Sedgwick, and *'Permanent, Faithful, Stable': Christian Same-Sex Partnerships* by Jeffrey John. Published by DLT 1992 and available from Affirming Catholicism, St Mary-le-Bow, Cheapside, London EC2V 6AU.
3 Quoted from *The Screwtape Letters*, 1942, p. 64. C. S. Lewis *The Great Divorce*, 1947, is an entertaining allegory of his understanding of what heaven, hell, and judgment might mean.

4 Catholic Persons: Images of Holiness. A Dialogue*

Rowan Williams and Philip Sheldrake

ROWAN WILLIAMS

This is a conversation which began about 21 years ago in Oxford. It will be a conversation about holiness. Not because we think we are experts in this subject, but because we thought that there is not much point in talking about being Catholic unless we try to make that pertinent to what our own wholeness might involve, and that is immediately to start talking about holiness, about sanctification. We hit on the title 'Catholic Persons' as a way of trying to hold that together, trying to talk about the kind of human being that Catholicism, Catholic Christianity rather, exists to foster; what the processes are, the disciplines and the images and imaginings that go to make Catholic persons. Hence the subtitle, 'Images of Holiness'. So we decided that I would tell you what 'Catholic' meant and Philip would tell you what 'persons' meant.

We have had a number of possible definitions of the word 'Catholic' already but I should like to pick up on something I have said in other contexts about the way in which 'Catholic', at least in part, has the sense of 'telling the whole truth'. I should like to think of Catholic spirituality as having to do with the way in which the wholeness, the fullness of Jesus Christ's story is made real in us. To struggle with the idea of Catholic holiness is to try to wrestle with the ways in which the whole story of Jesus Christ takes flesh, if you like, in me and you and in the

*© Rowan Williams and Philip Sheldrake 1993

infinite range of particular human identities that there are in the world. How does the story of becoming flesh, of announcing and being a sign of God's kingdom, of giving yourself into the hands of God, of bearing the cross, and living through the resurrection become particular here?

Baptism is the crucial mark of being Catholic and that is because baptism is about the paschal mystery: it is about entering into the Easter of Jesus and the exodus of Jesus. So, if we begin with this perception, that the wholeness of this kind of Catholicity has to do with the wholeness of the story of Jesus, we may have some boundaries within which to talk about sanctification, because for a Christian holiness is not just acquiring a kind of spiritual glow, it is not acquiring a high set of moral marks, it is not about having X, Y, and Z special experiences; it is about living Christ. What exactly that means is what we need to explore. How can the whole story of Jesus Christ become real in the wholeness of my humanity? There are all sorts of bits of my identity and no doubt yours as well which not only do not look very Christ-like, but look really conspicuously incapable of communicating Christ. There are the failures and the betrayals. There are the false, delusory hopes and aspirations. There are 'the things ill done and done to others' harm', as Eliot has it. There is the whole history of ambiguity and sin. Yet one of the rather extraordinary claims that Catholic theology makes about holiness is that actually all of this can speak of Christ, can become the way in which God speaks in Christ-like form to the world now. It has to do with that old medieval chestnut about the saints rejoicing over their sins in retrospect (as well as rejoicing in them while they were doing them, which is another story). But rejoicing over them in retrospect because they had been the occasion of learning and the occasion of grace and the occasion of mercy, and therefore become part of the whole fabric, all of which in each moment speaks of God and Christ.

Two sorts of wholeness, then: the whole of that pattern of Christ's story, the Son's course; and the whole of me. Holiness is those two wholenesses put together. And when you put them together, one of the things you realize is how little so many of our definitions of wholeness really have to do with sanctity. I come to this process as a deeply unwhole person who may never satisfy the criteria or demands of this or that psychological theory of wholeness, this or that projection of what it is like to be successful and good and nice and balanced and all those other things. I may never get quite there. On the other hand, I may get to be a saint.

That is the first point I want to make by way of introduction in talking about Catholic visions of holiness. Holiness means redeeming the whole of me. It does not entail all sorts of amputations of the bits I do not like, or repressions of the bits I do not like, but tries painfully and gradually to bring them all into the light of God's transforming power. And I would applaud very much what has been said about confession in relation to that transformation and the process of painfully bringing to the light the things we do not much like living with.

There is a second thing about Catholic holiness which I know Philip will want to say more about. In all this process of trying to bring the wholeness of me and the wholeness of Christ together, I always have before me the hope of transformation. It is ridiculous to think that I am ever going to get there and be able to say, 'Right, I have now brought these two wholes together and I can sit back.' Christ is always *to be* realized, *to be* made flesh in me and in us. That means that a fundamental part of being holy, or the road to being holy, or the process of sanctification, is *expectancy*, and perhaps one of the great marks of being holy is being *expectant*. Not optimistic or naïve about our hopes, but expectant, which means that the situations and the things and the persons we encounter are situations and things and persons that we approach in expectancy. We say, 'Now, how is this encounter at this moment going to assist in bringing Christ to life in my flesh?' The problem is posed very acutely particularly when I am with people I do not much like or agree with, and find difficult.

What are they saying to me of God in Christ, and how does that enter into my growth Christwards?

Behind this is a very basic, very crucial dimension of Catholic Christian thinking about human beings, which is, in a nutshell, the realization that my growth, my good, my welfare are never ever things in isolation. They are bound up with your growth, and your good, and your welfare, and if I think I can have my good without yours, then I have not really understood what the word 'Catholic' means. That is why it is so distressing when churches looking at one another, or people looking at one another within one church (naming no names) are willing to say, all round, 'Actually, we can do pretty well without you. My holiness, my welfare requires that you be kept at arm's length: that you be kept at arm's length from the Lord's table, that you be kept at arm's length from sacramental communion. My holiness demands your distance.' That really will not do for Christians: it is an appalling blasphemy and distortion of what Catholic holiness is about. And, of course, it is equally embarrassing for people who like to think of themselves as liberals and people who like to think of themselves as conservatives, because it leaves us stuck with the awful thought that, as Elizabeth Templeton puts it rather wonderfully in her book *The Strangeness of God*, 'Sooner, or later I am going to have to work out how I am going to get to heaven with Ian Paisley.' For 'Ian Paisley' read the person you find most difficult, the attitude you find most difficult, and you will see the point. It is not to say that we have no right to our discrimination, our decision, our self-determination. It is to say that, whereas we may conscientiously take a stand on this or that, that must not (and Christianly speaking, cannot) turn into an attitude that simply says, 'I take my stand, I define my good and my holiness in these terms, and for that I require that you not be around, please.' Somehow, that taking of a stand, that discernment and clarity and judgement which we all need, has to be held together in what looks at first sight like an impossible balance with the knowledge that, sooner or later, if I am to be reconciled with God, it is with and through those people who are so difficult and so obnoxious. This was expressed most dramatically, in a deeply suspect doctrinal way, by St Silouan of Mount Athos when he said that, frankly, he was not interested in getting into heaven as long as there was anybody else left outside. I think that is not just an expression of sentimental universalism, it is throwing into the middle of our thinking a real problem, to which I think there is no theoretical theological solution: a problem that our imagination must go on wrestling with.

There is a real sense in which the failure or the loss of another person is my failure and loss, and mine is theirs. Put that in terms of heaven and hell and, yes, we have a problem. Do not try to solve it; just let it worry you. I think that is what the best theological problems are for: not for solving, but for keeping us usefully uneasy. And that, of course, is precisely the point at which Catholic holiness has something very significant to say about our society. We are living in a society where, increasingly, it is not only possible, but positively recommended, that certain people think of their good and their welfare by ceasing to think of the good and welfare of others. We are coming to tolerate in this country, as elsewhere in the world, the notion of the underclass, the people who have no real stake in the way things are, and we are profoundly tempted (and I do mean 'we') to secure our comfort by simply blotting out the loss, the injury, the indignity of those who have no stake. Again, it will not do, because the Catholic vision demands that my good and yours and everyone's be held together, and this is a time when the idea that there might be a common human good – something that is good for all – is by no means as obvious as a particular kind of optimistic liberal might once have thought it was.

Those are just two sketchily-outlined preliminary thoughts on Catholic holiness: the two fullnesses. The fullness of what is myself, good or ill, and the fullness of the Son's course, the story of Jesus, being brought together. Then the inseparability of my good and yours: the way in which your identity, your loss, your gain, your struggle, your joy enters into and forms me as a believing person, and mine forms you.

PHILIP SHELDRAKE

I want to say something about Catholic spirituality, or the Catholic approach to spirituality; the Catholic idea of a personhood; and the Catholic idea of the human person. First a preliminary note. It seems to me that a rather important tension is held in any valid Christian spiritual journey. I mean the tension between rootedness and movement, between knowing where you are (or knowing where you come from) and knowing where you are going. Catholicity expresses boundaries in the sense that it is about saying, 'I know my place. I know my location.' But that location and sense of place is not a sort of magic chalk circle that you draw round yourself as some kind of protection against the powers of darkness (however or by whom they are expressed), so that if you dare step outside there is some awful sort of magical zap that is going to hit you. The importance of knowing your place is that, as an Indian friend of mine once put it, 'Only those who know where they come from are safe to journey.' It is being rooted in order to be able to journey. So I would also say that a healthy Christian spirituality is not only about knowing your place, knowing where you come from, but also about a healthy, non-possessive, non-invasive crossing of boundaries.

The three points that I want to make about my understanding of 'person' from a Catholic spiritual and theological perspective are these. First of all, as human persons we live, and we must try to experience ourselves as living, in a three-dimensional way. We live, as it were, within ourselves. Part of the journey is certainly into myself, to my own centre, seeking to appropriate more and more of the whole of myself. That is what you might call the 'intra-personal' dimension. But I am also at the same time, as Rowan very powerfully expressed it, in ultimate connection to that very process, exploring connections outwards

81

with particular others. That is what I would call the *'inter-personal'* dimension of personhood. But there is a third dimension, which Rowan touched on as well, which is that both my own exploration of myself, and my connections with particular others, all take place within a network – a matrix, if you like – of other, more structured, relationships. Not the ones I choose but the ones that are imposed on me, and which I can collude with, or I can protest against. This is, if you like, the social dimension of my existence. If we are talking about Catholic personhood and holiness, we have to take seriously this three-dimensional understanding of the person. Sheer self-awareness, or a psychologized version of spirituality that deals solely with me, is not adequate. It is necessary, perhaps, but it is not adequate. An exploration of particular human loves is also important, but that, too, is not adequate. It is only adequate if both of these find their place within an increasingly conscious and critical confrontation with the power of structures – the structures that I, and all of us, have to live within. This third dimension is constitutive, for better or for worse, of my person as well.

The second thing I want to say concerns inclusivity in relationship to 'the other'. How do we encounter 'the other', whoever or whatever 'the other' is? What kind of people (I think we need to think in terms of people particularly) do we experience as other or as, in some sense, over against myself? And what is my attitude when I do become aware of that otherness of people? Do I seek always for other people to be mirror images of myself? Do I seek to make them that? Do I push them away when they fail to be that? Or do I have a healthy sense of the uniqueness of incarnation in me, which liberates me to recognize the uniqueness of incarnation in you? In ecumenical dialogue, probably more ink has been spilt on the subject of the Eucharist than on any other. Much of it has been spilt on the subject of real presence. The most significant question about real presence, I find, is 'In *whom* do I find the real presence, and to whom do I refuse that recognition?' If I recognize the uniqueness of 'the other', then I am gradually going to be brought to recognize other particular kinds of real presences. I am going to discover 'the other' and all the others that populate my life as sacraments, the most potent sacrament of all before the two seven, ten, or however many medieval theology at one point thought there were. There is a multitude of sacraments, and they are called 'other people'. The grace they supply is strongly related to what Rowan said about one's own self-appropriation, and our approach to the other. What about what I experience as the broken other, or the other that does not fit the manicured, neatly packaged, version of human nature that I prefer to deal with? The degree to which I am able to own that reality in my reaction to other people has a very strong relationship to the degree that I can touch and own the darker edges of myself.

The third part of my understanding of personhood has to do with my own integration, but also it has to do with my attitude (or our attitude) to the world around us, to created reality, to the cosmos. A Catholic understanding of the person is also inclusive of all of me in the sense that it recognizes that I am graced nature. Not that I am spirit imprisoned in body. Not that I am body with some mysterious spiritual thing which is always slightly eluding my consciousness, or eluding my attention; but that I am an integrated spirit-body, or bodied spirit. I am not merely my body, but, equally, I cannot be most truly myself except as embodied. It seems to me that the much forgotten and little discussed (because what can one say about it?) Christian doctrine of the resurrection of the body is trying to say something rather substantial about the inherent reality of being human before God. Not a temporary, accidental reality, but an inherent reality of embodiment. Somebody (and I cannot remember who) described our own bodies and our bodily desires as God's own body language, and that is a very strongly sacramental understanding of embodiment. We need to listen to the language of our own bodies. The body, my body, your body, our bodies, are sacraments of our own identity; but also our bodies are sacraments of God's presence and reality to me. And that embodied spirit includes, as Rowan has hinted, even the flawed and imperfect and uncertain parts of myself.

Finally I want to suggest that a Catholic understanding of person is also about a subtle tension and balance between a legitimate self-possession and a necessary self-transcendence. The problem is that a great deal of classical spirituality (and I do not think Catholic traditions of spirituality were unique in this, but they certainly were quite potent) tended to provoke a premature self-denial, and it seems to me that self-denial and self-transcendence are not the same thing at all. A valid and a healthy spirituality is not about deconstructing the self. It is not about self-diminishment. Bernard Lonergan (a pretty dense theological mind, at least in my experience) did say something that I could get a grip on! He made the point that we cannot transcend the self until we possess the self to a legitimate degree. There is a legitimate and necessary self-appropriation that has to be part of the spiritual journey. However, the other side of the tension is that the person who seeks to be by clinging to self finds that that apparent self has already run through their fingers, that there is a difference between self-possession and, if you like, self-grasping. That is expressed strongly in the Gospel saying about laying down one's life in order to take it up: that the one who seeks to be by clinging to self like grim death, will find in any case that the self they thought they held has run out of their hands.

ROWAN WILLIAMS

Picking up on that last point, it seems to me that if we are to talk about 'God's body language' – a marvellous phrase – what we are saying is that God wants particulars, not generalities. God does not, you might say, create clichés. What is bestowed on each of us is particularity, one utterly distinctive way of being Christ-like. If that one distinctive way of being Christ-like is frustrated or denied, then something in God's communication to the world is frustrated and denied. There is a sort of smudge across the revealed face of God. When we see that particularity, that uniqueness in each one of us, for what it is, as a gift, as something God actually wants and longs for, then we have both the sense of that not being a possession, and at the same time, of that being immensely worthwhile. I actually have something to give. To use a phrase that means quite a lot to me, one of the greatest gifts that God gives us is to be givers. We all know this, I suspect, in personal and pastoral relations: to give the gift of being a giver is a tremendous lifegiving grace. By contrast, to keep someone trapped in receiving all the time from some great source of benevolence beyond them is dreadful and death-dealing.

Very practically, this relates to not only my willingness to give to others, but my willingness to ask from others. There is a kind of morality and spirituality, Catholic, Protestant, call it what you will, which is extremely wary about really asking, really talking about need, because somehow the ideal position is to be beyond needs, is it not? Somehow it seems to us terribly selfish to ask about our needs. And yet, if uniqueness and particularity is God's gift, part of what makes that uniqueness and particularity is the way other people feed into it. To be free to ask for help and for nurture seems to me to be closely related to holiness, not to be the opposite of it as sometimes you might imagine.

PHILIP SHELDRAKE

I agree, and I would link it with the way in which we understand God's relationship to us. It is a crucial point that 'God does not create clichés', God only creates particular people, God only relates particularly. If there is a universality to God's love, it is a universality of particularities. And that means, it seems to me, that the distinction between love as *agape*, a sort of universal, somewhat detached, non-passionate love, and the erotic, or *eros*, the particular love, the passionate love, the engaged love, is, as far as our relationship to God is concerned, quite invalid. On the contrary, it seems important that God

85

desires you, God desires me. We can't refuse the erotic, the passionate, to God. In turn, that says a great deal about the validity of my own sense of desiring. I remember somebody saying in a class some time ago, when I was talking about desire in the Christian tradition, 'I was always taught that desires were bad.' Then she paused and said (this was in America), 'Sorry, correction. *My* desires were bad. But Daddy's desires, the priest's desires, God's desires, my spouse's desires, those were what I had to listen to. In other words, *I* was not to be a person of desire.'

The way we see God relating to us, the medium of God's relationship with us, liberates us to recognize our own desiring. One of the ways, obviously, we come to find our desire is through a sense of neediness. We may well move from a multitude of surface desires or surface needs, gradually in and through them, to a sense of deep desire which is ultimately unanswerable through these things. But the point is, there is no short cut. You cannot dive straight into your deepest desire, you can't immediately become aware of what is ultimately your most profound spiritual aspiration. You have to work first with the sense of who you are, and your neediness. But if you are not free to ask, either of God or of the other, even at the surface level, there is no road into the deeper desire. And if there is not, then as I come to be a person (if we see personhood as a journey, not simply a static reality that you are somehow given in a package) there is a danger that that coming to be will largely be in relationship to extrinsic forces, rather than to the intrinsic reality of God within. If you spend all your life, as it were, coming to be in relationship to other people's desires understood by you as duties, then there is a real danger that the self gets constructed purely by reaction to outside influences. That is why being free to acknowledge and express desire matters.

ROWAN WILLIAMS

The word 'desire', and all that goes with it, is obviously a very slippery and difficult one, because very often we are encouraged to think of desire exclusively in terms of the ways in which we conscript other people into our self-definition, and say, 'I want you, because you must play that role.' That is sometimes so close to real deep need that distinguishing legitimate desire is desperately hard for all of us. I suppose it is something that anyone engaged in pastoral work knows a certain amount about, mostly by his or her appalling mistakes. The problem is to discern and deal with the often desperate need of another human being without collusion and falsehood and the kind of role-playing that just locks you into a particular pattern. And yet, even the worst kind of manipulation arises from a real need. Come to that, all of us, pastors or not, know something about the problem of dealing with the needy other person, and how very hard it is to disentangle the desire that is authentic from the superficial expression of it. But we can't do without the desire and love for the particular. One of the important things about it is that desiring and loving and needing this person, this reality, is what dispossesses us in a very important way, because it is where I stand conscious of my empty hands and my hunger. There is nothing I can do about it. I cannot plan my way round it or theorize my way round it. I guess that is really why, in the *Symposium*, Plato does, surprisingly in some ways, give such a colossal role to the desire of the particular other body. He says that is what educates you, because that is what brings you up short, that is what makes you feel the ache of lack and loss; whereas if you talk about desire for good or justice, or the love of the good in general, before you have been through that process, by comparison they remain bloodless desires, a set of relatively theoretical, manageable concerns. And whereas with the other kind of desire you may make a fool of yourself in all sorts of ways, and do all kinds of damage to yourself and others, the awful fact remains that this is where the dispossession happens, and therefore this

87

is where, somehow, God comes in. We do not, I think, come anywhere close to God without that sense of ache and lack and helplessness.

PHILIP SHELDRAKE

Yet so much of the Catholic spiritual tradition assumes that that kind of coming up against the other does not take place – or should not. I wonder whether there is a connection between the fact that spirituality so often became the possession of a celibate élite, and the need to create ascetical principles to substitute for what would otherwise happen in the normal process of personal relationships.

My other question is: Do you think there is ever a condition of fulfilment of desire and need? One of the features of a Catholic approach to spirituality is that the journey ends at some point: in union with God. There is perhaps a problem about whether the journey can begin without a degree of union with God, but there is always the expectation of an end-point (it may be far in the future, it may be an eschatological moment), but there is a point at which somehow all comes together. Is that the ending of desire? Is that the ending of need? Or is desire, this continual openness to possibility and to more, actually part of the condition of human relating to God, and always will be?

ROWAN WILLIAMS

It depends on what sort of God you believe in. If you believe in a God whose essence is finally expressible or containable, then of course you can have an end to the process. If you believe in a God who is not expressible and containable, the God with whom you are always launching out into the deep, then there is no possibility of talking about a goal, a finality. I think it is a strange, contradictory thing, to desire the ending of desire – to desire stasis, frozenness. There is much, to my reading anyway, in the Catholic spiritual tradition that constantly pulls against that static pattern, from St Paul and Gregory of Nyssa to Bernard and John of the Cross. The more you grow, the more there is to grow into. My primary school sermon illustration for this is a marvellous passage from C. S. Lewis in *The Voyage of the Dawn Treader*, where Lucy meets Aslan again after an interval. Lucy says to Aslan, 'You have grown'; and he says, 'No. You have.'

5 Holy Stardust*

Angela Tilby

Letter from America

I start with a letter from America. A picture of two educational institutions within a few miles of each other on the plains of Illinois, near Chicago.

The first is Wheaton College, a Christian school of higher education. Its mock Grecian architecture is reminiscent of Harvard, which it hopes to emulate. Here several thousand clean-cut, middle-class young Americans receive the last stages of a general education in a non-denominational, evangelical atmosphere. Wheaton is also a kind of reliquary for past Christian writers, many of them British. C. S. Lewis' wardrobe is interred here, as are numerous letters of Dorothy L. Sayers. You can't write a book about either without visiting Wheaton.

The other is a world-famous physics laboratory, Fermilab, built in the 1960s. Its central structure is a tapering tower of glass above the plain. In front of the main atrium, and underground, there is a circular tunnel four miles in circumference, where atomic particles are accelerated to speeds close to the speed of light and smashed into each other, in the hope of producing traces of even tinier particles released in the collision, which must exist in theory but have never been observed.

Both Wheaton College and Fermilab are in trouble. Wheaton is in trouble with its board of trustees. It has become too liberal over the years, and the conservative evangelical businessmen who hold the purse-strings and dictate the policy have appointed a new principal, a dispensationalist minister from a southern non-denominational church whose task it is to lick the place into shape. A third of the staff are delighted, a third are scanning the job advertisements, and a third are keeping their heads down.

Fermilab has never really been liked by the people of Illinois, although it has tried hard to be lovable. It has offered a classy, modernistic setting for concerts. It has commissioned sculptures. It even has its own herd of bison which thoughtfully chew the grass in the middle of the particle accelerator. Fermilab is short of cash, and no one has much sympathy these days with the esoterica of fundamental physics.

Wheaton College and Fermilab have nothing to do with each other. They might as well exist on separate continents. The new principal of Wheaton College is reported to have indicated that physics is not a priority on the curriculum as the return of the Lord Jesus Christ is so shortly expected. His task is to save Wheaton for the sake of the nation's soul, so that it is supplied with another generation of fresh-faced professionals who will make money as doctors and lawyers, remember their old college, and serve the Lord. Interestingly, he doesn't seem to expect much trouble from Wheaton's science department. The rumours are that if there is a purge it will begin with the theologians. They are real trouble.

Nor does Fermilab rate theology very highly, though I always have to remember a remark that a British physicist made to me, that physicists think more about God than do the clergy. But Fermilab does not need theologians. It is, after all, a temple to science. A mighty bronze and gilded pendulum swings through a sandpit in the atrium, somehow reminding the visitor that he stands on sacred ground. Beneath his feet the secrets of creation are laid bare. In the control room, in the days leading up to the projection of a photon or electron beam, the atmosphere is tense with excitement and concentration. Nobody here can really believe that the administration would be so foolish as not to go on funding research of such monumental importance, in which the honour of the nation is at stake. Here, the indignity of the W and Z particles being found in Europe, at the accelerator at CERN, is still remembered with bitterness.

I start in America because it provides a nice example of the fragmentation of a culture. Not only do Wheaton College and Fermilab know nothing about each other; you get the impression that neither wants to know. Yet both institutions face difficulties with cash and with credibility. Both could also be said to be dealing with the things of God: Wheaton through a Bible-based curriculum curiously isolated from the philosophical and cultural milieu in which it is set, though willing, no doubt, to use television and computers and the benefits of technology which have been produced within that matrix; Fermilab through a quest for the fundamental nature of physical reality. The assumption is that if you understand the physical you have understood everything, for the nature of the universe is physical, and there is nothing else. See Wittgenstein's gnomic saying at the beginning of the *Tractatus*: 'The world is that which is the case.' So the physicist's quest is to find *what the word God has always been a substitute for*: in other words, the ultimate equation which explains everything without remainder.

Neither institution has much room for each other. Once they might have been rivals, in the sense that there might have been an argument between them about which view of the world was truer. But now the two tasks, the two narratives about reality if you like, run alongside each other without meeting. (So it is with all our narratives, science, faith, politics, art, call them what you will.)

What do the dilemmas of Wheaton College and Fermilab say to Catholic Christians? Especially those who describe themselves as 'Affirming'?

Affirmations of creation

One of the great affirmations that I have found in Catholicism is that of the reality and goodness of the created world. That needs a little teasing out.

As a teenager I absorbed a form of evangelical religion in which the natural world was construed as so fallen, so depraved, that it could not be trusted to reflect the character or purpose of the creator. Whether it was nature itself that was fallen, or our inability in our unregenerate state to reason properly about nature, was never quite clear. Take Calvin, for example, who glories in the splendour of God's creation; God's laws and ordinances, even the harshness of suffering, as an expression of God's goodness. Our failure is that we don't see it. Sin blinds us to the righteousness of God. A different kind of evangelical religion includes a streak of protest against nature itself. One thinks of the writings, say, of the blind poet Jack Clemo. He portrays the Christ of Mark's Gospel, commanding the storm to cease. The winds and the waves obey him, and cease from violence. Nature in itself is fallen, recalcitrant, subject to frustration.

The two strands that evangelical faith inherited had profoundly different pastoral consequences. Was the answer to suffering submission or protest? Was John Wimber right to counsel David Watson to hope for healing from his cancer, or should he have helped him face up to the terminal nature of his illness?

I found some resolution as I began to read the early Christian fathers. I was genuinely surprised, and delighted, to discover that it was very much part of the early Gospel to proclaim the unity of the world, and its rationality, in the context of a culture in which neither were obvious.

To the man or woman in the forum it might have seemed much more obvious that there was a balance of conflicting cosmic powers struggling for superiority. Or that there were higher and lower levels to creation pulling us in two directions. Or that nature was somehow a botched effort

93

by a flawed craftsman. It was possible then, as now, to espouse a pure materialism, in which mind and soul are to be explained wholly in physical categories; or a pure spiritualism, in which matter is a kind of illusion.

It was this world of differing and competing cosmologies which the early Church addressed. Not directly, with the message of Jesus Christ, his call and his kingdom, but with an interpretation of the universe. This was the proclamation that all things were made by God, and are in themselves good. That all men and women are called to live according to their rational nature. That whatever is wrong with the universe, and with us, is held within God's overall design for good, and can and will be redeemed. That God's reason was always present, immanent in the creation as the *logos*, which was now born into the world as Jesus Christ. This was the preamble to the Gospel; the world view which the Gospel itself both presupposes and helps to create in a kind of circular feedback loop of insight.

The early Christians were engaged, at least in part, in a public relations exercise. They were thought of as a particularly nasty group of people, fanatical, obsessed with death, unattractive in every respect. They had to make a case for intellectual respectability. But the emphasis on creation was not only designed for pagans. There was a real need to meet the cosmologies of the day, to enter and engage with the philosophical world-views which permeated society.

There were other interpretations within the Christian world which denied the goodness of matter, cutting Christianity off from the deepest insights of the faith of Israel. These interpretations, Gnostic or Marcionite, were no doubt compelling to those who followed them, as the beliefs of the New Age, with which they have much in common, are today. Gnosticism despairs of creation as it is, in its earthiness and ambiguity. It looks for paths through the aeons; for the bodily disciplines which flatter and console, for the spiritual massage which brings inner harmony and outer serenity. But mainstream Catholic

Christianity did not accept Gnosticism, however much it may, at times, have absorbed its dualistic spirit.

For Catholic Christianity the Gospel of God comes first. There is no point in a redemption that leaves out the world of matter, that dissolves away the gospel into psychology, however profound and absorbing. Catholic Christianity has to consider the wholeness of things, the meaning of matter, of bodies as well as minds, physics as well as metaphysics. It aims at a greater connectedness than the Gnostics allow.

The early fathers were not afraid to enter into an argument with Hellenistic culture to justify their fundamental convictions. As it turned out this was fortuitous for the development of science in the West. There is a good case for saying that God was the single unifying principle that made science possible. The birth of Christianity meant that for the first time the Greek fascination with reality was brought into alignment with the Hebrew belief in the Oneness and otherness of God. There was an immense simplification in the belief in One rational God, who was not identified with the universe. It was possible for the first time to look at the world, to observe it in the expectation that it would behave in regular and predictable ways.

Theologians began to observe nature, to enjoy it, in the expectation that it was alive with messages, coded clues, moral warnings and hints. St Basil of Caesarea, for example, writes of the sea urchin as 'a little contemptible creature'; nevertheless, God has 'impressed on this little animal a manifest proof of his own wisdom'. He has watched the sea urchin and noted its capacity to cling to rocks in spite of the clawing tide, giving a signal to sailors of an impending storm.

Sometimes the beauty of nature is clothed in longing and regret, as in the writings of Augustine. The visible world grieves us with the memory of the goodness we have lost and the distance we have yet to travel to heaven. But whether the mood is ecstatic, curious or wistful, the attitude is anthropocentric. Everything is made for human beings, who are the peak of God's creation. The doctrines of creation and incarnation are inextricably linked in Catholic Christianity. The whole creation points towards the human, mature and redeemed in Christ. The status of human beings is judged on the basis of our creation in the image of God, and by the fact that the Son of God took on human nature.

Science and religion

It is in this light that we ought to see what is at stake in the conflict of science and religion that arose out of that movement of European thought that we now call the Enlightenment. It was not simply about the literal truth of the Bible nor that science threatened to make God redundant. What was really at issue was the centrality of the *human*. We can see this in the earliest of struggles: that between the Catholic Church and Galileo. There was nothing heretical *as such* in the idea of Copernicus's heliocentric solar system which Galileo propounded. What the Church really objected to was Galileo's attempt to establish measurements and relationships between physical objects in a purely disinterested way. In other words, to put the human mind outside nature, to establish the reality and constancy of the world apart from and independent of human beings. Those who condemned Galileo were right in so far as they perceived that the denial of the human would in time alter everything that could be said about God, leaving us with a bare choice of an inhuman God or no God at all.

It is a strange irony that the Catholic Church has vindicated Galileo at a time when many scientists are coming to the view that mind itself and the kind of beings which have minds like ours actually belong in nature in a fundamental way, and cannot be separated from it.

The outcome of Galileo's condemnation was that research into fundamental physics and astronomy could not go on in Catholic countries. The scientific enterprise passed to countries where Reformation teachings were accepted. Here, where creation was construed as more theologically opaque, where the creation–incarnation axis was replaced by a theology of the revealed word of God and the centrality of the Cross, there was less of a conflict of interest between science and religion.

It must be said, however, that the great scientists of the sixteenth and seventeenth centuries were devout men, awestricken by the wisdom of God revealed in the order of creation. The important point is that it was theologically defensible for them to look at the universe as a closed system, created and controlled by the divine mind but uncontaminated in its essence by fragile, warring humanity.

The greatest of the Protestant scientists was Sir Isaac Newton, the discoverer of the laws of motion and of gravity, and of work on the nature of light which only came to fruition this century. Newton belonged to the Church of England all his life, but he was a secret heretic. He didn't believe in the Trinity or the Incarnation. He was a plain man, his spirituality had a Puritan streak to it, scrupulous and obsessive, and he hated Roman Catholics. He also hated priesthood and ceremonial. (In the seventeenth century science appealed to Puritans and dissenters, who disapproved of classical learning because of the sexual cavorting of the Greek and Roman gods. High churchmen, Catholics, tended to look down on science as an inferior discipline, for the uncultured. This was the beginning of a kind of spiritual snobbery which still exists among many Catholics, both Anglicans and Romans, the heirs of F. D. Maurice and those that read *The Tablet*. It manifests itself as a basic suspicion of technology, engineering and their fruits in commerce and trade.)

Newton's universe was a mighty machine in which stars and planets, light, and every particle of matter were bound together by inexorable but beautiful divine laws. It was a vision that was spiritually fruitful in its time, reinforcing the idea of God's control of things, which was important in a troubled and turbulent age. The God who held the stars by gravity could be invoked with confidence to 'order the unruly wills and affections of sinful men' and 'still the outrage of a violent and unruly people'. Newton's cosmology finds a curious parallel in the liturgical writing of the Book of Common Prayer, with its strong emphasis on a right ordering of our conduct, its sense of the smallness and fragility of humankind in the face of the righteousness of God, our helplessness in the face of the inhuman machine that is the natural world, a place of storms, failed harvests, awful weather, lustful instincts and all manner of greed and bestiality.

It is fashionable these days to condemn Newton as the source of all that is wrong with Western science and technology, to implicate him in the failure of Christendom to live at peace with the earth and with other species. To do so is to forget the magnificence of his vision and its capacity to liberate energy, both physical and spiritual. The roots of Newton's vision were in a God of astonishing order, calm, and reason, whose response to us is both wise and swift and inexorably just. Newton's God was born of protest against the wars of religion, against superstition, intolerance, and the hurling of dogmatic slogans. We forget the great spiritual courage involved in his detachment. To see the universe as it is without humanity at its centre is an austere quest, as searching as that of Buddhism when it insists on dissolving as an illusion the experience of the self.

What happened in the Enlightenment changed the content of our imaginations. Newton's new physics provided the framework of a new way of grasping what it meant to live as creatures in space and time. Newton gave boundaries and certainties to the imagination because he believed that space and time were constant. The constant of constants was God, who guaranteed the cosmic order by standing, as it were, outside the universe. God was, in his own being, absolute space and time and volume. He was absolutely necessary to physics. God had a place to be in. Admittedly, there was no real, absolute space – in Newton's universe nothing rests, everything is in perpetual motion. But the rate of motion, the distances, the forces with which bodies interact with each other, are completely measurable and predictable.

We absorbed Newton into our spirituality as a kind of puritanism and distance, both from our own bodies and from all bodies, and, of course, from God. We lived as discrete beings who attracted and repelled one another but could never really get inside one another. We lived as restless beings, driven to work, driven to become, to improve, produce, succeed. Sometimes faith took on these characteristics. Sometimes faith set itself up as an alternative to them and concerned itself with feeling and interiority. Faith occupied a role inside the self rather like the 'angel of the house' – the Victorian wife and mother, who guarded the sacred hearth while father was away doing his business in the cold, dry, harsh world of the intellect and the machine.

We absorbed Newton into our theology as a reductionist search for the purest, earliest, simplest, and most direct version of the faith. We searched the Scriptures looking for the essential units, the primitive atoms, if you like, to be distinguished from the forces of history, culture and tradition which had artfully, and artificially, beaded them into chains of meaning.

We absorbed Newton into our politics and our sexuality in a belief that history would run in straight lines if only we found the right opening moves, that deviance from the norm was either corrigible or incorrigible but never a genuine variation, as there is only one straight line possible between two points. Always in the back of one's mind are the little golden clockwork spheres circling the sun on their predetermined metallic tracks.

But physics and cosmology have not stayed with Newton. We now have to respond to a universe that is no less awesome but more complex and more subtle and diverse than Newton could have seen. It is not surprising that we now experience Newton's God not as a liberator, as he was in his time, but as an oppressor, a tyrant. That flowering of revolt that we see in feminist theology and elsewhere, crude and immature though it often is, is

99

carrying the charge of a dreadful knowledge that Newton's God is now a mask, and not the glass of vision through which we can perceive something of the edge of the form of the likeness of the True and Living One.

The new science strips God of his enlightenment attributes, and for many of our contemporaries atheism is the only rational option. We suffer in their hostility and indifference. Our spirituality is driven into Gnostic byways, false alleys promising a false wholeness which numbs the pain of our fragmentation. Our moral life is all in pieces as we seek a new order of being to fall out of the physics. What we need to take on and discern theologically, spiritually, and liturgically is how this universe which modern science discloses to us can be celebrated as God's creation. So turn away and consider the stars, the seas and the creatures. I find I am compelled again and again back to the book of Job, to contemplate the whirling storm centre where Job found God, when his cosy moralism was stripped away by a suffering he had not desired but which stalked him until he was forced to his strange repentance.

Order The first thing to say about this universe is that it still rests on basic beliefs about the regularity and orderliness of nature. The monotheistic principle, that the universe is one, is still basic to science, and we couldn't do science without it. This is a universe, not a diverse. But Newtonian certainties have been superseded in three specific areas.

Relativity The first is that Newton's notion of absolute time and space turns out to be an illusion. The universe is, in the language of Einstein's General Theory of Relativity, a space–time continuum. Time and space are wound up together, so that we can almost say that time is a dimension of space. There is no 'outside' for God to live in, because space is no longer seen as a kind of box or container with all the things of the universe in it and God outside it, marking the edges. God is either in and out of everything or in and out of nothing.

Then there is the discovery which we also owe to Einstein (to his Special Theory rather than the General one) that matter itself is a form of energy. The particles of which the universe is composed and the forces which act on them are not separate things. Everything is interlinked and interrelated. We are not isolated discrete entities, but indissolubly connected to everything else. Whatever else this does, it frees us from false dualisms. We are embedded in nature; we are ourselves microcosms of the universe, complex structures of matter and force.

Indeterminacy   At the same time the old division between the observer and the observed, the objectivity and detachment on which science has rested, has been shown to have limits in the discoveries of quantum mechanics. Quantum mechanics is the measurement of interactions between particles at the subatomic level. Very early on it was discovered that there is a limit to what we can know about the behaviour of subatomic particles. If you set up an experiment to discover their speed, you exclude the possibility of knowing their position, and vice versa. What the experimenter decides to find out helps to determine how the particles behave. Subject and object are intertwined in a way that is quite foreign to the physics of Galileo and Newton. Newton's belief that measurement was ultimately a process which could be controlled by detached observers has been proved false. We can have a dialogue with a subatomic particle, but we cannot tell it what to do.

Quantum mechanics is not a weird kind of esoteric philosophy – its fruits are all over our world in the everyday technology of television and computers, aeronautics and lasers. It has immense practical application. Quantum mechanics is about calculating probabilities, not certainties. What this suggests to me is that at a very basic level the universe is constructed with a surprising degree of flexibility and freedom. You could say that the foundations of *choice* are laid down before the foundation of the world.

101

I think this explains something that we find in modern spirituality and approaches to pastoral care. When we hit problems in our life or when people come to us with difficulties, the language in which they are expressed has less to do with right and wrong, deviance and guilt, and more to do with identity, with choice, with how to be the self one is. If the questions that hang over Newton's physics is *Where am I? How am I moving?*, the questions that shadow us from modern physics are more *What am I?* and *How can I be?* This is especially so since, extrapolated on to the grand scale, the origin of the whole universe is now usually thought of as a product of quantum processes. A bubble of space–time pops out of a vacuum and blows itself up with such speed that elementary matter is pulled into being. It is, as the physicist Alan Guth has put it, 'the ultimate free lunch' – or, in the language of Irenaeus, a primordial act of grace. It all might not have been. Or it might have been other, a universe which flew apart or collapsed in on itself. Instead, we have this majestic stability and creativity, welded together by gravity. The constants on which the world rests are very precise, very finely tuned. A God who creates, imagines, designs such a universe is a God who looks for partnership, for response, who is prepared to take the risk of disaster. Not, as Freeman Dyson put it, 'the best of all possible worlds', but perhaps the most interesting.

Chaos Then lastly there is the fascinating new science of chaos. In Newton's universe everything is predictable. The discovery of chaos theory is that nature does not work like Newton's machines. Chaos is the science of the unpredictable and so is concerned with things like British weather, the stock market, volcanoes, snowflakes, the patterns formed by clouds, or the trajectories of washing blowing on a line. These are complex, everyday realities with behaviours that cannot be predicted accurately. What can be said about them is 'lost in a storm of complexity'. Chaotic systems are everywhere in the universe. They exist in nature much more frequently than Newtonian predictable mechanistic systems. In fact, it has been said that Newton's systems are abstractions and idealizations from nature, giving us models from which we build machines. But the real things in nature dance to a different drum. They are described by equations which can't be run backwards. Non-linear equations which never resolve, and can only be displayed by moving images, fractals on a computer screen, like the sea or endlessly opening petals, or lava, a pattern which is always different and always the same.

If nature is more like this than it is like a machine then it does help to explain the push in nature to develop new forms, to experiment and try things. Always the same, always different. The pack of basic ingredients is endlessly reshuffled. If chaos theory is right, then the whole story of the evolution of life becomes something which can be understood. Human beings have often been portrayed in the philosophy and literature of this century as lonely, shipwrecked aliens, but contemporary cosmology suggests that we are not an anomaly in this universe. We are not strangers here, but pilgrims. Chance becomes one of the tools of change, and not the arbitrary, meaningless accident that it has become in our thinking.

One advocate of chaos theory likens the themes in nature to a grand Bach fugue. The original notes may be quite few and simple, but they are played in a particular order and then developed. The harmonies change, the theme diversifies; here is the variation that builds, here is the unexpected one, here is the grand climax and the ending in a place which is clearly related to the beginning, but could not have been foreseen.

The architect of all this change and creativity is *time*. Both Newton and Einstein assumed that time was not fundamental to nature. For them, the true nature of things was timeless. But in the new physics, time is architecture, time is shape and form. Time is experiment and direction.

Enhancing the theoretical insights of recent physics are the recent startling discoveries about the actual universe we live in. And the discoveries here have been startling.

We do live in a historic universe, a universe that has been created. It does not last forever. It has changed and will change again. This is a universe of process in which time has a creative function. The order which we discern in the universe is not an eternal order but an emerging one. Our very existence depends upon the atomic reactions that occurred billions of years ago inside stars which then exploded, spewing their contents out into space. We are linked to the stars in every cell of our bodies. Many of the elements which make up our bodies were not present at the beginning of time, but were created in the deep furnaces of stars.

Whatever else this does, it should enable us to honour that sense of history and tradition which is part of our Catholic heritage. Nature and history are not separate things. The universe has a history, a visible record of catastrophes and new beginnings, of violence and stability. Development is inevitable, and so are huge wrenches from the past. There is a sacrificial principle at work in nature, in which life feeds off non-life; the rubble of a star creates an animal. Nothing is lost, but everything is changed. Change and transformation; 'making these things other', as David Jones put in in his great poem, the Anathemata, the sacramental principle, the Eucharistic principle, is already at the heart of the created world.

Of course, this also leaves us with new and agonizing questions. This universe is a violent place, there is gratuitous suffering along with grace – in fact, it is the flip side of it. So there is a cry that comes to us about, *How can I suffer? What does my suffering mean?* Suffering is not anomalous in this universe, but inevitable. How do we honour the evolutionary dead ends, the freaks and monsters, who have their part in our world's story? Again, for many of our contemporaries, the anxiety raised by these questions is so great that atheism is the only comfort and consolation.

Yet it remains true that none of this could be recognised or appreciated or suffered without a new evaluation of the place of *mind*. What is becoming clear is that there is a limit to the project by which mind is excluded from the universe. There is an astonishing congruence between our minds and the way nature seems to work. Nearly all scientists accept this congruence quite placidly, without always reflecting on how extraordinary it is. Why should we, chancy creatures on a remote planet, be able to calculate so exactly and accurately what is going on in an interaction between particles too small to observe except by the faint traces of debris they leave behind in a collision? Why should we have the concepts of number that match what happened in the earliest microseconds of the universe? Non-scientists, especially in this age of cultural relativism, sometimes assume that science is a way of making things up, projecting the contents of our own heads on to nature. But that isn't how the scientist sees it, or how nature seems to behave. There is a sense, not of invention, but of discovery; that the relationships created in a particle collision are really there, that we have stalked the elusive quark, and discovered something that was always there waiting for us to give it a name.

This is a new kind of anthropocentrism, one that sees mind as congruent, not alien to nature, which is taken for granted by scientists. There is no genuine remoteness in this universe, however huge it is on the cosmic scale, however tiny on the subatomic scale. Everywhere is central.

So this is the kind of world we live in. Ordered and united. Seamlessly interlocking. In some sense genuinely open and unpredictable, sculpted by time.

Our contemporaries know enough about all this to find both our hesitancy and our peremptory certainties baffling and unconvincing. We could say, of course, as they say at Wheaton College, that all this is rather unimportant since the Lord is returning soon and will wind up this whole system, having rescued the few believing souls who are destined for eternity. Or we could say that the processes of nature have nothing to do with the doctrine of creation, which is grasped by faith and not by reason, and therefore

105

has nothing to do with the mechanisms discovered by science.

Or we could say piously that the attempt to engage with contemporary cosmology is a form of intellectual idolatry, and that any talk of God which does not translate immediately into human concern is false. While there are people starving we have no right to do fundamental physics, let alone to enjoy it, or to enjoy thinking about its consequences.

We could follow the Sea of Faith movement in finding the universe revealed by science so hostile and meaningless that God can only be conceived as an inner. psychological reality, a human creation. The objective world is so frightful that God cannot possibly be responsible for it. Let us locate him in the mind as the source of our values. No matter that in a universe such as ours there seems to be no such distinction between inner and outer, physical and psychological. If there is no 'outside' for God to inhabit, there is no 'inside' either.

When I think of those young men and women at Fermilab, I see a group of people who are disciplined, quiet, and strangely humble as they wait for the moment of the beam and for what it will reveal. They are not trying to save the world, but to listen to it. They know that if they get the fundamentals right, the applications will come. But to pressure the thinking process by the demand for relevant results is to cease to be attentive to the thing itself. There is more of a contemplative spirit in Fermilab than in the anxious activism of contemporary Catholic life.

On the whole, however, we collude with the fragmentation of our world, inventing cosy ecclesiologies which condemn technology and science in order to keep our naïvety intact. We are very talkative about injustice and the need for healing, but fail completely to acknowledge our own depression, marginalization and unbelief. Our mission to heal is ridden by unacknowledged guilt and anxiety.

Where are the apologists who can interpret this world to our contemporaries? Where is the Austin Farrer? Why did John Austin Baker write only one major book of Christian apologetic? We needed ten. Working in the mass media, I am surrounded by colleagues who are concerned about the world, who live spiritual lives, but for whom the Church and committed faith are matters of total indifference. 'If it helps you', they say, 'go for it. I prefer aromatherapy.' It hurts that my good, honest pagan friends assume that Christian belief is merely a form of personal psychotherapy, and has nothing to say about the world as it is. I worry for my feminist friends who are seduced into paganism because they have never heard that women are made in God's image.

Consequences

I believe it is necessary for Catholic theology to engage with contemporary cosmology so that we are dealing with truth and not illusion. I say this because I believe that one of the main reasons people don't go to church is that they don't regard the Church's beliefs as true.

I think we have spent too much time trying to be judged useful in a disbelieving world. Too much time translating our faith into politics or psychology, so that the world picks up the message that our beliefs are only held in a symbolic, reductive way, they have no substance, no real connection to that which is the case, the swirling atoms and the stars.

A Catholic theology of creation must begin with contemplation. With remembering the words of the *Jubilate*: 'Be ye sure that the Lord he is God. It is he that hath made us, and not we ourselves.'

6 Catholicism in the Future. A Dialogue*

David Jenkins and Lavinia Byrne

DAVID JENKINS

The whole business of being a bishop in the Church of England at the moment can be extremely distasteful and troubling; when the said bishop says he is going to retire, and then has a holiday, he has time to think and ask himself, 'Well, what the hell is it all about?' My experience of this is that it is very closely related to my being deeply, desperately, and yet hopefully concerned with Catholicity. Let me try and quickly – in existential shorthand – explain why.

In a way it all began when I was a boy. I gave my heart to Jesus at a certain rally. I had discovered that there was this God around who was for me, and that seemed exciting. But I had no idea how exciting it would become, because, of course, I went on to learn that this God who was for me was the God for all. And the thing became more and more excitingly focused for me in the glories of the Holy Trinity – this God who is greater than great, more loving than love, closer than close, and is concerned with absolutely everything. Hence, a Catholic Church, worshipping the one universal God, sustained by the sacraments of the universal Gospel, and committed to this universal mission. You see – quite simple!

Well, it is; it is absolutely simple. It is how you face the complexities on the basis of the simplicity which matters. And this brings me to the crux, which I think is also a

*© David Jenkins and Lavinia Byrne

crisis or judgement and a *kairos* or opportunity. The crux is that this universal mission is to share in the sharing of God. It is not to build and protect a sort of pro-empire for God called the Church. We have got to rediscover, or rather, by God's grace, to be rediscovered and recaptured by this understanding that what it is all about is sharing in the sharing of God. What gets in the way of this seems to me increasingly to be the idolatrous model of central-ized Church authority. It is true that the Papacy looks like one extreme case of this, but I think it spreads much wider, which is why I regard this dialogue with Lavinia as about asking how we both, from our different positions and perspectives, face this problem. The problem can emerge as ecclesiolatry, bibliolatry, or what I might call guru-olatry or charismatolatry. But they all resemble one another in making people think they have 'got it', and that the focus is here, that it is certain and assuring, and that it somehow has to be protected by all sorts of fences.

But now we have this immense urgency of newness, or rediscovering the calling of the Church in regard to the mission of God at a time of both *crisis* and *kairos*. The judgement seems to me to be clear, especially for the Church here and now. It is shameful that we so often in the Church present things in such a way that people who are seriously concerned about things in the world, people who are seriously seeking, simply cannot bear with it. We live in one world. It is one threatened world, and it is one threatening world, but it is also one glorious world, and desperately looking for one source of being, salvation, fellowship. Is that not what the Catholic Church is, or should be? Is it not our task, a very urgent and down-to-earth task, to rescue these claims about Catholicity for the call about universality?

Catholicity seems to have been diverted by some of its most vocal proponents into a tradition based on a deposit, something which is sometimes rather narrowly defined and historically confined, instead of being understood as a calling based on a gift towards the future. The more you look back, the more you get dragged back into the past instead of using the tradition for enabling increasing openness, which is part of God's eschatology, God's future. Of course, I am concentrated very much nowadays on eschatology because I spend half my time either preaching at funerals or at memorial services to my colleagues. And it is right to take that cheerfully, but it is a very real issue. Where are we going? And why do we go on discussing obsessively all these stupid and neurotic questions when the world has so many demands and when the Gospel is so glorious? So I look to Affirming Catholicism as being part of this exercise, part of this calling, to rescue the word 'Catholic', which has somehow become a party word and turned inwards, into being a missionary word turned outwards and heading for the universal future of the universal God.

LAVINIA BYRNE

What pleases me most in what David has just said is that he has opened a question about the place of authority. He has not gone for the jugular and attacked named individuals about positions they hold. Every time I go to Ireland I struggle, particularly when I go to Belfast, for I am so intensely aware in that environment of the baggage attached to the Catholic label. Here I am now sitting behind a large label that says 'Affirming Catholicism', as though Catholicism were necessarily and simply a good word. But it is not, and it has not always been. It has got an upside and a downside. I think we should be quite clear about examining both sides, so that what we take forward into the future is the good bit, and so that we work very cautiously with the downside of our history and see if we cannot transform it.

Let me tell you what I mean. I collect second-hand books, not just casually, but obsessively. So I will go into the most Protestant bookshop I can find in the north of Ireland with my courage in my hands, because I know, as my mother says, that my hair looks Irish. To you it would not indicate anything, but to the people in that bookshop it proclaims straight away that I am an Irish Roman

Catholic. So I go in the door and I say, 'Can you tell me where the Huguenot section is, please, because I want to find out something about my ancestors?' Then their panic level subsides somewhat, and I can continue my voyage of exploration. Actually, my password is true and enables me to affirm some of my own Protestantism. Some of my ancestors were, indeed, those Huguenots who left France at the revocation of the Edict of Nantes and found security in County Fermanagh. The upside of their Protestantism enabled them to leave one country in the name of religious tolerance and the freedom of their conscience; when they got to Northern Ireland they became flax merchants, they made linen, they settled down, they became burghers and lived happily ever after. And eventually, irony of ironies, became Roman Catholics! It seems to me that Protestantism too has the upside of the call to individual conscience, the call to integrity; but a downside too in that tendency to turn into solid burghers and live happily ever after. So you can speak of the two sides of Protestantism as well as the two sides of Catholicism. In Catholicism you might speak of the upside that is about universality, and the downside that turns people into gurus and which, instead of treating the papacy with respect as a source of teaching and authority, turns it into something which can command too much of the authority of our own consciences.

Only this week a woman was woken up in the night to find her husband shot dead in the bed beside her. I find that, as an image of religious conflict, a horrendous metaphor. People are killing each other about these words, these labels. As we go forward into debate, let us do so seeking clarity.

Another story from Ireland. I was at St Patrick's College in Drumcondra with some Methodist women over the weekend, and the chairman of the Methodist Conference in Ireland came up to me on the Friday evening and said, with tears in his eyes, 'I have a photograph of the feet of Mother Theresa of Calcutta. Her feet were photographed recently in Dublin, and they remind me of Dürer's praying

111

hands.' I wanted to say, 'How obscene. How horrible.' Because it seems to me that every time we turn other people into saints, we deny something of our own saintliness. I am reminded that Mother Theresa herself, when a journalist put a microphone at her face at our airport and asked, 'Are you a saint?' replied 'Yes. And so are you.'

When we talk about questions of authority or leadership in our Churches, we must do so in a way which empowers our own leadership, our own holiness, our own sense of discernment, and the gift of obedience, which means listening. The Pope is as bound by a pledge to obedience as I am and as you are. It means a pledge to listen – listen to the voices clamouring out for attention in the world. And let it be said about the present Pope that he has put the human person back centrally on the map. You may not like the way he has done it. You may be troubled by some of his insistence about legislation on abortion and the rights of the foetus, or against birth control, but it could be that he is right. So, as we begin to talk about the future, do not let us do so from a position that merely bashes, but let us do so in the exploratory style that David's remarks have enabled us to take.

DAVID JENKINS
My immediate response is, 'How do we find the way forward?' What do we pick up out of this which addresses our understanding of God's revelation and command to us? And which addresses two other things: first, the voices that come to us from the world, to which we ought to listen, and second, the confused and confusing voices which we are all hearing about authority. We are confronted by the question of authority to ordain women, the question of authority in morality, and focused in the leaks about *Splendor Veritatis* and the way people have reacted rather hysterically to them. You raise the question about moral authority with regard to abortion, the Pope, contraceptive methods, and so on. These are all areas of listening, and I believe that if we can listen in dialogue and in fellowship God will speak to us through it. You know,

there is not just one voice of God. He has started reson-
ances in the Pope, and in the Protestant conscience, and
in the Bible, and, of course, in the tradition. But the world
is also a place where he is speaking to us, and I also think
he is speaking to us in our own anxieties and confusions.

Your mention of the human person seems to me to come
very near to the centre of it (and I do not think that is
just a self-centred conclusion, I think it follows from the
Incarnation and from our being in the image of God). It
is persons we ought certainly to be concerned with. So
how do we 'federate our concerns'? It seems to me that
so many of our discussions are confrontations. The minute
anything is said people want a row in the press or to
confront one another. What I mean by 'federated' is related
to what made me very ready to do this dialogue, because
I find that when I sit down with people there is trust, both
between people and some bigger trust in God which is
over us and under us. Yet so often we do not seem to be
able to bring it out, because somehow we do not trust
enough, in God, it seems to me, to overcome our mistrust
of one another.

LAVINIA BYRNE
The key word that sprang into my mind when you began
talking is the word 'discernment', though sometimes we
use it so loosely that it can become yet another of the
buzz words that rise and fall at the moment. The spiritual
tradition I come from could not be more Catholic. I was
baptized in the font at the Birmingham Oratory by a priest
called Father Dennis Shiel, who had been admitted into
the Oratory community by Cardinal Newman. He was the
final novice whom Newman admitted into that community. Father Dennis married my grandparents, married
my parents, baptized all of us. You see what one is offered
by that? An enormous sense of security. Security to be
absolutely honest, which means that I am totally comfort-
able with the word 'discernment', the process of being
open to ideas, listening and weighing up. I think, too, you
have put your finger on something particularly important

about the labels we use. The example you chose was the ordination of women to the priesthood, and the word that flashed through my mind was 'secular'. We were told at the time that a lot of the arguments that were being used were purely secular, and 'secular' was used as a nasty word, was it not? Yet secular only means 'of the age', and if God is not revealed in our age, in the warp and weft of our daily concerns and communications, where is he? So it seems to me the task is to listen as part of a discernment process. Not simply to label and dismiss out of hand and out of order those bits of the Church that we cannot bear, or those voices that we despise.

I went into one Protestant bookshop in Edinburgh where the owner said to me, 'Are you saved?' (and this was at 9.30 in the morning!). I said, 'I hope so.' He said, 'Well, that is the difference between you and me, because I know so.' And I thought, 'Oh, I know about that from inside myself. How tempting to have that level of certainty, those kinds of answers.' But that is not what I am called to. I am called to the dispensation of trust, which commits one to grow in belief. So I am glad I began with Newman's font, because it was Newman who said, 'A living idea becomes many, yet remains one.' This came home to me when I took part in a seminar with Rosemary Radford Ruether about six years ago at Heythrop College in London. What I retained was her repeated insistence that 'The fullness of Christian truth lies in the future, at the *eschaton*, at the fullness of the age.' It does not lie in the past, so we are not constantly involved in archaeological work. It seems to me that wherever she has moved now, that was a profoundly Catholic insight. Ours is a call forwards, not a call backwards. So how are we to start discerning? How are we going to listen to the voices of this world in an authoritative way without just handing them a rhetoric that no longer works?

DAVID JENKINS
It will require serious acceptance, in our guts as well as in our heads, in our spirits and in our relationships with

114

one another in decision-taking bodies in the Churches, that this business about the future is of critical importance. Fullness of truth lies in the future; we have not got there yet. The fullness of the Church lies in the future; we have not got there yet. And it is certainly related to what you were saying about security. I was trying to think where I would get mine from. This is possibly to reveal myself a total cheat as far as the public prints go, but I have never doubted that God has given himself for me. This also brings us to Affirming Catholicism in, shall we say, a narrower sense as well as a broader sense – because I want to say that for me this has very rapidly become connected with the sacraments. If I am in a state of insecurity – which I very often am – and especially since I have been a bishop, in a state of depression (well, you see, as a bishop you are open to everything in the Church instead of being able to dodge half of it, and the things you come up against *are* threatening), then I just have to testify, I go to the celebration of the Eucharist, the Holy Communion, and there is the givenness repeated. There it is, and I do not have to argue about it. Of course, I may at other times need to argue about the history of the Eucharist and the way people interpret and misinterpret it. These are necessary complexities that come up in practice, just as you have to think very hard about explaining something in a confirmation service according to the people who are there. But the sheer simplicity of the givenness is *there*, and it requires a body, an institution, a continuing corporateness which is in some way both authorized *for*, and authorized *by* this givenness.

LAVINIA BYRNE
What is Anglo-Catholicism going to do, then, to put in place something that is the equivalent of a second Vatican Council, to demand of you appropriate change? Particularly, what are you going to do to get rid of that image which appears to care only what length candles are, or how deep the lace is? I remember hearing on the radio, after the debate about the ordination of women, something

to the effect that certain priests were considering leaving the Church of England and coming over to Rome, and I groaned inside myself that they would be so disappointed. On the second Sunday of Advent, I went to Mass in a Catholic church in Durham. At the beginning of Mass the priest said, 'Because it is Advent, symbolically there will be no lights on. And, by the way, the children are receiving their first Holy Communion books today.' So, at the offertory in they came, these little six- and seven-year-olds, waving their books, and they all went up for individual blessings. Throughout that Mass we sang the most chronic hymns from the seventies, and at the end I was introduced to the priest, who said, 'There were three of them in church today.' So I said, 'What do you mean?' He said, 'Three of them, you know, Anglicans, who are thinking of coming over.' And I said, 'Well, if you keep up the present liturgical standard . . .'

I tell that story against various constituencies, but I tell it in order to provoke all of us to ask, 'What is a good way forward liturgically?' Anglicans could learn much from some of the trashing that has happened in the Roman Catholic community over the last 30 years. Certain things we have got rid of too quickly. Certain things we are finding it quite difficult to replace. Because Anglo-Catholicism at least partly seems to have been in a kind of time warp, I hope you will begin some sort of liturgical reform as part of what you are grasping as the educational process of Affirming Catholicism. How can you do so in a way that frees up the basic, essential simplicity of the sacraments, so that they not only meet our instant need and greet us as people of desires, but also touch what was mentioned this morning about the sacrificial spirit that is at the heart of creation? How can all of that be celebrated?

DAVID JENKINS

Part of the answer would be, if we could work out why it is we are having such a good time at the moment. If you go away and think about it, each of us is being kicked in a particularly delicate place somewhere in our guts about something that we are discussing in this Conference, but somehow we are also able to laugh, and that makes it all work. I wonder what it is that has made us so very solemn when we come to synodical discussions.

I feel very strongly we are frozen by a lack of trust. Real trust would enable us to relax with one another, which could help with this whole business of discernment. The point about discerning is that it must have, it seems to me, an element of waiting, attending, to pick up what God wants us to see. Discerning does not mean waiting until I get a bright idea and then rushing on with it. It must be related to a responsible accountability to the tradition and a responsible sharing in the scriptures. These things must come together to get any effective discernment. But what we seem to do so much in the Church of England, because of the unfortunate way Synod has developed, is to set up something like a parliamentary adversarial debate. And I do not see how you discern what God wants us to see, or from one's own end what one can pick up and offer to God, in adversarial ways. I think the adversarial instinct is partly related to this false certainty. People seem to think that if you really believed and were really concerned with God, then, by referring to your authority, you would know straight away what the answer is to any question. Instead of which it is really that the body has to live with these things, until the right thing emerges; and that is why we need one another. Why cannot we move forward in a more relaxed sense?

I have recently been involved in discussions about keeping people together in the Church of England in the aftermath of the November vote, and of course the notion of impaired communion and all the rest of it throws certain people into a panic. But is there not a real communion, if I may put it so, simply in the name of Jesus, which we can trust while we work out these very sticky questions? We seem to have become so solemn and defensive about it that consensus is almost precluded from the first. It does seem to me that, if we are going to go forward on this, we really are going to have to confront what I think I

117

must call our respective idolatries. Because the point about an idol, both in religious matters and in economic and political matters, is that so often an idol is a good turned into a god. And when you turn a good into a god, then you expect more of that good than can be delivered; because a good made into a god becomes an idol with feet of clay. So that the good of the assurance which scripture gives, or the good which comes from having a real sense of belonging to the community which God has called you into, or the good of the experiences of God which you have had yourself, or whatever at one point has been a helpful means to God, can end up replacing God and becomes an idol. I feel increasingly that if we are going to work together for the Catholicity of the future, we are going to have to challenge one another seriously and to challenge ourselves about our respective idolatries. But it is really up to each of us, or each of us in our community or our group, to challenge our own idolatry, rather than other people's, so that we can carry things forward.

LAVINIA BYRNE

Isn't it interesting? You can sit there and say you have problems with the General Synod. I, who belong to a Church that does not have a General Synod, look at it and say, 'Gosh, wouldn't it be wonderful to have a place where people got together and even had adversarial conversations?'

It would be very nice if all groups were discerning groups, but I do not think they need to be. When I look at certain of our Churches, I am so attracted by what they represent, and by their method, which is the consensus method. But I sometimes wonder if the model of the Trinity behind that method is not a Modalist one. Modalism is the heresy that describes the Persons of the Trinity as being three different aspects of the one God. I do not believe they are. I do not believe that God has three different modes for being with us. I am rather more orthodox. I believe in three different persons in the blessed Trinity, with the consequence that you could theoretically have a conflict of interests within the Godhead. Consequently, it is all right for us to be put into contexts where what is required of us is more than just consensus. When I looked at your debate last year I thought, 'My God, I cannot believe it. These guys are going out through different doors. That is fine. But they are expected to come back in and sit down together.' And that made the hair stand up on the back of my neck. Not only that you should be required to hold different positions from each other in a broad Church, but that you should be required too to come back and form a group, a Church, a community together, even though you know you hold different opinions. It seems to me that that is, if you like, a far more ambitious project than consensus, and it is one where the demand on Christian charity goes far deeper. Yet ideally, I respect the fact that if that group could also be a genuinely discerning group, sharing and weighing conflicting perspectives, it would be much, much better, because it is not simply about arguing one's corner. It is about trying to listen to one another in order to listen to the voice of God.

DAVID JENKINS

Yes, of course, it must be 'both/and'. I find what Lavinia has said immensely encouraging and moving, especially at this moment of my calling and the calling of my colleagues in the House of Bishops. Because in our poor, stumbling way, we have been deeply concerned to find some way of enabling people who really disagree, who genuinely and profoundly disagree, to hold together. And we must face the fact that the disagreements are real. I get tired now when people on either side say, 'Oh, you have not listened to us.' Because on either side the answer is (I fear it has to be faced) that we are rejecting what you say precisely because we have listened to you and we cannot in conscience agree. That is the point about this mucked-up phrase 'the two integrities', which is quite wrong. You cannot have two integrities about views, you can only have different people who hold different views with integrity. If the views clash, one of the two views is wrong, but it can

119

still be held with integrity. This must be so. Otherwise you have hypostasized integrity, whereas what we are talking about is people, people who can and must approach things with integrity, hoping to be moved into the wholeness of God.

I have become increasingly of the view that in trying to wrestle with our common incompetence, people like me who are fairly clever with words are liable to justify anything if you give us long enough. So one wonders sometimes if that is the game one is playing. (And what is a purple shirt for, after all?) But I think not, and I hope not. If God is God, the point is not our mistrust of one another, but our common trust in God, and finding where it takes us.

LAVINIA BYRNE

I want to pick up on something that has been running in and out of everything we have been saying. What are we doing to put the good news before people? Let me quote a sentence to you: 'Who shall presume to put my candle, which God has lit, under a bushel?' It was said by Mrs General Booth, who wrote a book on female ministry in the middle of the last century. It actually began, 'Who shall presume to cast women out of the Church's operations? Who shall presume to put my candle, which God has lit, under a bushel?' When I was editing that collection of writings by women called *The Hidden Tradition*, I was moved by the fact that it was those great evangelical women, like Mrs Booth, with their empowering and passionate language, who actually spoke to something deep in my Catholic imagination. Equally, 'Jesus, the very thought of Thee' could have been written by Wesley, and of course Newman began as an evangelical. When you talk in that kind of language, I resonate with it because it has a directness and it reminds me of my own self as a source of life and as a recipient of life and light. So, somehow I would hope that in all our discussions we, in our affirming of Catholicism, will affirm our receptivity to that rather simple language, and those rather simple insights that enabled hymns like 'Jesus, the very thought of Thee with sweetness fills my breast' to be written and to be sung.

DAVID JENKINS
This gives us an immediate clue, because we need to be able to pick up some things that can be of practical use in this struggling towards an open agenda, and in tackling this central issue of what we are doing to share the Gospel. It is a question which should be asked all the time alongside things like, 'What do we have to do in order to preserve this, or protect that, or, above all, carry on the other?' Certainly things do have to be preserved, and this is one of the reasons for being concerned, it seems to me, with affirming Catholicism in some form or other; things do have to be protected, carried on. These are perfectly proper concerns. But they must not be defining concerns, not least because, unless God carries them on, we have had it anyway. So it seems to me that a lot of the questions which have got mixed up with defining Catholicity or Catholicism are perfectly proper questions, but they are, strictly speaking, secondary questions. They are questions which get on to the responsibilities that we have to exercise, but they must not be allowed to define the situation totally, and I think this comes back to where I started. I get a terrible feeling that, in so many of our activities at the moment in the churches (and I think it goes all the way from the Vatican to Lambeth), we do look as if we are confined and defined by these questions without asking the primary question. The primary question, it seems to me, goes in two directions: first, how do we actually worship God, and second, how does this enable us to share the Gospel? If what we are discussing, and the way we discuss it, is getting in the way of the worship of God, or sharing the Gospel, then our priorities are wrong. At the same time we cannot be naïve. It is quite clear to me that you cannot do without the Church, and hence all the issues of Catholicity, authority, and so on. How the hell do you live with the fact that most of the time you

121

cannot do *with* it? But this is a question to laugh with, because sin will not have dominion.

LAVINIA BYRNE

While you were talking I was reminded of a Jesuit priest, Michael Kyne, who used to talk about the Church as vehicle and the Church as obstacle. But I do not think it stops simply with the Church. I think it is true, probably, of all of us. We are both obstacle and vehicle to the transmission of the Gospel. What I should like to see us all doing is claiming some authority for the Church, as well as hounding it and reminding it of all the myriad ways it gets it wrong. The Church could be a good – a better – vehicle for grace, a vehicle for communicating the Gospel. And so, too, could we be, but it would be useful to sort out what belongs to the Church and what belongs to us in all of this.

It is easy when you are a Roman Catholic, because the Church means 'them in Rome', and 'us' means 'Catholics in England who, if we keep our heads down, will be able to live happily ever after!' I wander in and out of that word 'Church', and as a member of a religious order it is so much easier to do, because you have the order you belong to, and that is your primary level of belonging in a curious way. So if you have a nun who gets in a spot of trouble in the Philippines, she can be airlifted out and hidden in County Clare for three months before she then pops up again in southern India. The religious orders, particularly the international ones, enjoy that kind of fluidity and able-to-move-on-ness. But that is dodging the question. Because, of course, as a Roman Catholic I am a member of the Roman Catholic Church and the Church is me as well as the people I talk about as if they were 'out there'.

DAVID JENKINS

Do we not have to develop that? I suspect this is an issue that requires further practical investigation, in particular this issue of belonging. We are talking around an issue of practical spirituality which is to do with what you might call 'relaxed and relaxing belonging'. Is it not one of the dangers of the way in which Catholicism has been expressed, in this very strong hierarchical way, which makes it so easy for you to think of 'them' as the Church and us here? And are we not challenged, especially on the Catholic side of things, by the proper role, the full sharing role of the laity, to make it clear that we are all the Church, we are all 'us'? Do you not think that the notion of a specially authorized class or caste which by virtue of their hierarchical position has determinative authority, is to be strongly and rightly undermined? Undermined because of the behaviour of such authoritative castes and classes, because it does not really reflect the body, if the body is to be the body of Christ; and undermined because of the way in which it actually disempowers and incapacitates people from being their full selves and their best selves in Christ. I do sometimes think that all the Churches, but especially the Churches which have laid a special claim to being Catholic, are under the most severe judgement at the present.

I was at a meeting of the House of Bishops some little time ago, when we were earnestly discussing matters of sexuality. I suddenly gazed up at all these elderly gents, and I thought to myself, 'This is totally absurd.' It was like R. H. Lightfoot, who once preached a sermon on joy in Queen's College Chapel, which was one of the gloomiest sermons I ever heard. Somehow the disjunction with reality comes over you, makes you feel the absurdity. Here we were, this collection of the middle-aged and elderly, including me, getting ready to pontificate about sex, which many of us were past and many of us regretted. There was something simply inhuman and stupid about it, that authority should be thought to reside in such a gathering in that way. As with Lightfoot's sermon, the message is belied by the deprived humanity of the messengers. The fact that the Church has produced this state of affairs demands a new Reformation. This is so serious a matter, one might almost say psychologically, and certainly with

123

regard to mission and preaching and serving, that this I feel is one of the reasons why, at any rate within the Church of England at the moment, the decision to ordain women is crucial. It goes terribly deep.

LAVINIA BYRNE

In parenthesis again, I would like to say that one of the problems I see around the ordination of women is that too great a charge is going to be laid upon them. They are going to be expected to be superwomen who will suddenly sort out all your Church's problems. What we should all be aspiring to, it seems to me, is the renewal of ministry. If ordaining women is part of that, then roll on the day it happens in my Church, roll on the day in all our Churches, right back to those that began ordaining women in 1916. But that is not the only answer. Somewhere along the line is the question of finding the authoritative voice of the individual, of the group, of the laity, of each of us within the Church. I believe it was at the First Vatican Council that somebody said 'Who are the laity?' And he was told 'You would look pretty stupid without them.' We forget that to our cost.

That is why I would return again to that question, Where is your Second Vatican Council? Where is that thing that has said to you with the authority of the papal document, of the council document *Gaudium et Spes*, 'the joys, the hopes, the fears, the anxieties of the people of this age are the joys and hopes, fears and anxieties, of the person of Christ'? Where are you setting up the mechanisms for producing something that can listen to those joys and hopes, fears and anxieties? Otherwise we might as well all pack up shop, because the renewal of ministry is the renewal of the desire in everybody to proclaim the good news. It is back to the simple evangelical language of St Bernard of Clairvaux's hymn, 'Jesus, the very thought of Thee with sweetness fills my breast'. How are we going to find a way of saying that nowadays?

DAVID JENKINS

I feel that a probable clue here is by returning to simple thanksgiving as part of our spirituality. It is there liturgically, but so many of us, it seems to me, have lost the ordinary practice of it. If Jesus is Lord, if his death and Resurrection means that God will not be defeated, even by us, then our basic approach to life should be thanksgiving. Thanksgiving, among other things, for the Church. I think that we need very strongly to reaffirm this in simplicity and in simple dependence upon God. Then there follow these questions of relaxed belonging. It is only in fellowship and communion that our current problems can be taken forward, and in the renewal of this sense of belonging for something joyful, something joyful which may lead you into painful uncertainties and involvements, but where there is this dependence upon God he will bring newness out of them.

This sense of belonging requires us to work out ways of enabling one another and listening to one another across the boundaries. Perhaps because I am now nearly at the end of my seventh decade, though I started by being very worried, I find myself feeling one almost should not worry too much about these worries, because it is going to take time, is it not, to move forward to whatever God wants next. So we need thanksgiving, belonging, enabling, and listening, which leads back to expectancy. We seem much of the time in the Church to have given up expectancy. We are only hoping to survive, almost. Whereas in fact there is a glorious future. I often think that the glorious future will come when the Church of England is finally broken down and some of us will be able to break out. You never know, do you, how God is going to make or re-make things? But it will not happen easily, or without pain.

LAVINIA BYRNE

I detect at the moment signs that people who have never met a nun or a priest or a religious person are actually beginning to ask religious questions. I was at a book award

ceremony for the Fawcett Society, the campaigners for
women's suffrage, during which I gave a talk about what
religion had done for women, both the pluses and the
minuses. At the end of it a woman of about 35 came up
to me and said, 'I have never heard anybody talk
religion to me.' Now you could say, 'Well, where has she
been for the last 35 years?' But think about it. Her life
marks the time during which our religious educators have
gone through a crisis of confidence, and it is quite possible
that she has not heard. It seems to me that popping up
all over at the moment there are opportunities to evangelize people who have never heard the language of the
Gospel. I went to the hairdresser's six months ago and
the young woman washing my hair asked, 'Where do you
work?' I said, 'On Lower Marsh, in the big church building.' She said, 'Yes, my great-aunt was in the Bible.' I
looked a bit baffled, and she said, 'Yes, she was. Gladys
Aylward.' And I thought, 'My God, how tragic.' Gladys
Aylward left school at 14, worked as a parlourmaid, and
was able to save up her fare to go and evangelize in China.
In two generations we have gone from that situation,
where a woman could be totally empowered by the Bible
to change her life, to one where her great-niece is totally
ignorant of who might or might not be in the Bible. And
it seems to me that much of what we spend our time
doing, all of us, in my Church and your Church, at meetings like this, is messing people about who actually
deserve something better of us. So let us do this work,
because it is important, but let us do it so that we can go
out and actually have something worthwhile to tell people.
And let us do it with joy, which is a mark of the Holy
Spirit.

DAVID JENKINS

It is obvious that we share so many things. The question
we have got to live with, and live joyfully with, is 'What
are we doing to share the Gospel?' The encouragement to
do it comes not merely from within the Gospel, but from
the many people who are searching. There are so many

people around who go on caring about things like justice and injustice. I have come to call them the threefold Cs: the carers, the cursers, and the campaigners. There are the people who care so much that they set out and continue campaigning and trying to do things. But the people who protest, whom I call 'the cursers', are also very important people, because they are reacting to real outrages. Some of the people I have come across who are mostly militantly atheist are really cursing in anger against the world which God seems to have inflicted on them, or conversely, because the people who they think ought to show them God do not. And you can pick up signs of people who are caring or cursing or campaigning, so there are plenty of people to share the Gospel with. We cannot shirk it because of the political preoccupations that we were talking about. I do not think there is any short cut through these preoccupations. What counts is the way you contextualize them and get inward to the simplicity and outward to the demands of the world. The last point that I should like to make is that I think people do recognize something like a mixture of holiness, integrity, and concern if it is given to you. Of course, if you claim to have it, it is a lot of nonsense. People who set themselves up as saints or prophets are hellish. I always felt sorry for a certain clergyman friend of mine who suddenly became known as being good on the Holy Ghost. It nearly wrecked him. But, none the less, people who will let themselves go for the joy of God, or who just confront realities and have a go, are amazingly recognized, supported; and somehow we have got to build this into the whole life of the Church and subordinate, but not dodge, all the other difficult questions that we have got to live with. We can't get out of them. But they are not the main thing.

7 Forward in Faith*

Richard Holloway

When I was twelve a little cousin who lived up the street from us died of meningitis. This was in 1946, the year after the war ended. Her father, my namesake, was still abroad with the navy. We lived near the school I attended and it was normal for me to come home in the middle of the day for lunch. That morning, however, my mother told me to go to my cousin's house, where she'd be comforting the bereaved mother. While I was there, eating my soup, the rector of the local church came in to arrange the funeral. He asked who I was and commanded me to appear at church on Sunday to enrol as a server. It is hard to get inside my own mind as it was then, to relive the now of then, but I don't remember any particular reluctance about obeying him, though I'd never been a church-goer before. My mother was a believer, though not until later a great churchgoer. All I could testify to was a sort of implicit agreement that there was a God to whom we were somehow related. What experience I'd had of church was pretty boring, though the kids in our street frequently attended the local Ebenezer Chapel, mainly because they gave us tea and Paris buns after the lantern slide shows. I had no idea what to expect at St Mungo's. Father Mackay, the rector, was a very advanced churchman and he had converted this middle-of-the-road congregation into an Anglo-Catholic shrine. On the altar there was a tabernacle, flanked by six candles. Incense was used at worship, and

128

after Evensong on Sundays there was Adoration of the Blessed Sacrament.

I knew nothing about any of this when I made my way to Burnbrae, to St Mungo's, the following Sunday. When I got there I fell in love with it all. Looking back, I can see that it was an aesthetic conversion. I was converted by beauty. I had only the haziest idea about what it all meant or what religion was about, but I was captivated by the mystery and the beauty of the liturgy. I can remember the excitement with which I learned to use the missal given to me by Father Mackay. I was particularly captivated by the woodcuts that illustrated the book, especially the woodcut for the Feast of all Saints. It showed a priest at the altar elevating the Host at Mass, while behind him knelt the deacon and sub-deacon. Above the altar, with its six proud candles, there were companies of angels adoring the lamb that stood on a cloud, below a triangle representing the Trinity, directly above the elevated Host. I hadn't a clue what it all meant, but it spoke of something tremendous and other-worldly and I was captured by it. I don't know whether I was susceptible to holy places before my first visit to St Mungo's, but I have certainly been susceptible ever since. In my youthful ignorance I was captured by the sense of the Holy, the otherness, the beauty of God. I didn't know the lines then, but I'd clearly come to one of those places that are the world's end, in Eliot's phrase. I'd looked across the frontier and caught a glimpse of the beauty of God.

In my untutored way I was experiencing the primordial element in religion, which is adoration of the sheer Godness of God, the beauty of God. In the beginning, before theology or morality or the institutionalizing of the experience, human beings are drawn to God for God's own sake. They fall in love with God. That's what had happened to me. That primary experience strikes me still as being truer, less studied, than anything else that succeeded it in my encounters with Christianity.

Eighteen months later, when I told Father Mackay that I wanted to become a priest, he arranged for me to go into the Cottage at Kelham, where they tried to train uneducated boys like me for the ministry. By this time I had been confirmed and knew a bit about how to serve in the sanctuary, but I was still ignorant about Christianity as a whole. I can distinctly remember going up to the rectory the night before I was due to leave for Kelham, aged fourteen. I wanted some kind of comfort and reassurance, because I was already feeling homesick at the thought of leaving Scotland. I picked up a Bible in Father Mackay's study, but didn't know how to use it. I had a sense that I could find some comfort in it, but did not know where to look. I opened it at the beginning of the book of Genesis and read the account of the Creation, from which I derived no consolation whatsoever.

I'm glad now that I found God before I discovered the Bible. The Bible is difficult. Is it a holy thing in itself, the dictation of Almighty God to be taken neat, or is it a human construct and therefore a flawed reality containing both good and evil, genuine insights into God and ugly projections of human craziness? It has taken me years to find the confidence to make choices in scripture, to dig through the rubble, to glimpse the sketch of the face I know. I call this searching for the Gospel within the Gospel, looking for the Bible within the Bible. The lectionary I've been using this summer has taken me through the Books of Samuel. They were as full of incident and crazy humanity as the thrillers I was reading. I was intrigued by the number of times scripture tells us that 'the anger of the Lord was kindled against Israel'. In chapter 24 of the Second Book of Samuel we are told that God incited David against the people of Israel saying, 'Go, number Israel and Judah.' Having completed the census against the advice of Joab and the commanders of the army, David's heart smites him and he confesses to God that he has sinned greatly in what he has done, and asks the Lord to take away his iniquity. The Lord sends the Prophet Gad and offers David three choices: three years of famine in the land, to flee three months before his foes while they pursue him, or three days' pestilence. David chooses three days' pestilence, 'and there died of the people, from Dan to Beersheba, seventy thousand men'.

I'm still not sure what that's all about, though a natural- istic interpretation would suggest that David, in a fit of egomania, wanted to know how many subjects there were in his kingdom. The endearing thing about David is his self-doubt and realism. Did he connect a particular out- break of plague with his own guilt about the census, or is there something even more mysterious going on? It's a strange world to enter but it does have its familiar echoes. When Absalom rebels against David his father and pro- claims himself king, during the time of his brief reign in Jerusalem he is advised by Ahithophel, ' "Go into your father's concubines, whom he has left to keep house; and all Israel will hear that you have made yourself odious to your father, and the hands of all who are with you will be strengthened." So they pitched a tent for Absalom upon the roof; and Absalom went into his father's concubines in the sight of all Israel.'

There are echoes there of the rapes of the Muslim women in Bosnia. A feminist hermeneutic would point out that the rape of the concubines was a power statement, not a sexual act, that treated the women as a means through which ascendancy was claimed. Before I leave the Second Book of Samuel, let me remind you of the glimpses we get of another woman. This one with a name, Michal, the daughter of Saul. She's mentioned about nine or ten times. We are told that she was Saul's daughter, who was given in marriage to David. Something of her personality comes through in the scanty references we have to her. She's one of those strong women in the Bible whom the system ultimately defeats. When Saul turns against him Michal assists David to escape, and during his years in the wilderness, pursued by Saul, we are told that 'Saul gave Michal his daughter to Paltiel, the son of Laish.' After the death of Saul, David, now King of Judah and negotiating for the crown of Israel, demands the return of his wife Michal. This was probably a dynastic rather than a romantic claim. We are told in 2 Samuel 3 that

131

'Ishbosheth sent, and took her from her husband Paltiel the son of Laish. But her husband went with her, weeping after her all the way to Bahurim.' There are two further mentions of Michal in 2 Samuel. When the Ark is brought back to Jerusalem David dances before it and Michal, we read, despised him in her heart. When David returns to his household Michal comes out to meet him and says, 'How the king of Israel honoured himself today, uncovering himself today before the eyes of his servants' maids, as one of the vulgar fellows shamelessly uncovers himself.' And David said to Michal, ' "I will make myself yet more contemptible than this, and I will be abased in your eyes; but by the maids of whom you have spoken, by them I shall be held in honour." And Michal the daughter of Saul had no child till the day of her death.'

One of the things the new feminist hermeneutic is bringing to our appreciation of scripture is a reassessment of incidents like that. While I was in the United States in 1993 I read a sermon by a black Baptist minister, a woman who runs a self-empowerment group for women in the ghetto. She preached about Hagar, another strong woman in scripture defeated by the system, whose plight speaks to us down the ages. The point I'm coming to is that scripture in all its mystery and offensiveness needs to be interpreted dynamically. It is not something that is sacred in itself, something that can be used without an interpretative system. We need a hermeneutic of development if it is to mean anything to us in these days.

I should like to suggest that the Bible offers us its own key for interpretation. The Bible is its own best critic. It points us to the Bible within the Bible, the God beyond God. The key to it all, it seems to me, is the warning against idolatry. It is there throughout scripture, right up to the Letters of John. It tells us insistently, 'My little children, keep yourselves from idols.' My incompetence with scripture used to be more than tainted with irritation at this theme. The fear of graven images in the Ten Commandments seemed to me to be unCatholic and the constant denunciation of Canaanite religion, with its appealing fertility symbols and attractive visual aids, seemed to me to be ungenerous in the extreme. I disliked the idea of a jealous God, because jealousy and cruelty seem to me to be the ugliest of the vices. I can see now that I was reacting to the surface of things and that my late twentieth-century political correctness was blinding me to the real story behind all the divine spluttering in scripture. Idolatry is our biggest danger.

Let me try to define what I mean by idolatry. Idolatry is to absolutize the relative, to finalize the contingent. It is to take something that is created and offer it a loyalty that nothing created can bear. It is to give divine authority to things that are not divine, even though they may on occasions have been instruments of the divine. Idolatry is a process of objectification whose aim is control of the divine. This is why Pablo Richard, a Latin American theologian, writes:

> Evangelization must direct its attention mainly to idolatry, not to atheism. The oppressive world of today is a world of fetishes and idols, of clerics and theologians. The modern capitalist system is growing more religious and pious by the day. Heightened scientific and technical production has been accompanied by an even greater production of gods, cults, temples, and religious and theological symbols. Atheism has become a serious problem for the capitalist system: it is an obstacle to the production, circulation, and consumption of idols and fetishes.

An idol in a consumerist culture establishes and consoles one in slavery. Pablo Richard goes on: 'They refused a God who would rescue them from slavery: they preferred one who would live with them in slavery. . . . They wanted God-consoler-in-oppression and not God-leader-out-of-slavery.'

The motive for idolatry is understandable. It comes from our anxiety and insecurity, our inability to live by the uncertainties of faith, our loneliness before the elusiveness of God. An idol is the objectification of these needs and anxieties. The classic text on idolatry is Exodus 32, in which we read of the people's impatience with Moses and the demandingly elusive God he represents. During one of his absences on the Holy Mount, the people gathered themselves together to Aaron and said to him, 'Up, make us gods, who shall go before us; as for this Moses, a man who brought us up out of the land of Egypt, we do not know what has become of him.' Aaron takes the earrings from their wives, their sons and their daughters and fashions them into a calf and says, 'These are your gods, O Israel, who brought you up out of the land of Egypt.' The idol consoled the children of Israel, because it was a controllable object, something they could possess. They exchanged the loneliness and freedom of the real God for an idol that consoled as it enslaved. A subtler form of the same impulse is found in 2 Samuel 7, where we read that King David felt guilty, because he dwelt in a house of cedar, while the Ark of God dwelt in a tent. 'But that same night the word of the Lord came to Nathan, "Go and tell my servant David, 'Thus says the Lord: would you build me a house to dwell in? I have not dwelt in a house since the day I brought up the people of Israel from Egypt to this day, but I have been moving about in a tent for my dwelling. In all places where I have moved with all the people of Israel, did I speak a word with any of the judges of Israel, whom I commanded to shepherd my people Israel, saying "Why have you not built me a house of cedar?" '

The longing to objectify the divine, to rescue God from the nomad's tent and establish God in a permanent house of cedar, is dangerous, precisely because it answers so deeply to our needs. The sacramental genius of Catholicism is an aspect of this. I have already indicated how much I owe this system. It was through the sacramental richness and visual imagery of Catholic liturgy that I encountered God. God comes through this tradition. God uses the house of cedar as well as the nomad's tent. God visits them, tabernacles in them for our sake, but never permits the divine nature to be confined by them.

The flip side of the Catholic sacramental system has

always been its tendency towards petty idolatry. I have been in sanctuaries tyrannized over by obsessive MCs, for whom Ritual Notes was a more important text than the Sermon on the Mount, and a departure from ceremonial tradition more culpable than a breach of the Ten Commandments. This is an ancient tendancy that is intrinsic to human nature. It lies behind the anger of the Pharisees at the freedom of Jesus with regard to the Sabbath. The Sabbath was not itself holy, Jesus pointed out. It was made for us that through it we might be made holy, but they had turned it into an idol that constrained the very compassion of God.

This idolatrizing dynamic is a permanent danger for the Church. It is inescapably related to the Church's task in the world. The first duty of the Church is to bear witness to the Gospel and share it with the nations. This inevitably involves the Church in creating structures that will embody the Gospel, make it accessible in time and place; but this need for structures is also our greatest danger.

In the Christian movement several things are always going on at the same time. There is the primary task of the gathering of a people. We have a new message for humanity. In Christ, God proclaims a new thing, a new understanding of the Divine nature as unconditional love and eternal mercy. Those first captured by this message are compelled, by its sheer power, to share it. They go out into the world as heralds and proclaimers, sharing the good news of what God has done for humanity in Christ. They gather people, they make converts, they create communities. Then two things begin to happen. They have to care for and organize the people they have gathered and so shape them that they in turn can go out and be themselves heralds who bring the good news to their generation. But something else is always going on at the same time. We are talking about the creation of a Church, the gathering of a people. However, this Christian reality, this divine institution, always and unavoidably reflects and parallels the surrounding culture. The Church, which is meant to reflect the mind and mercy of God, also begins to reflect

135

the world and its best or most fashionable political structures. During its most formative years the Church was
surrounded by intensely authoritarian structures and it
has, to a very great extent, interiorized their understanding
of institutions, their paradigm of government. We operate
like a mini state, with a government and laws, values
and customs, and a particular intellectual culture we call
theology.

More and more we realize that this theoretical model of
the Church as unchanging authoritative truth and undevi-
ating institutional permanence is comically at variance
with the reality we all live with. Indeed, we could go
much further and say that the model we have borrowed
from the state no longer works for the state either. Part of
the anguish of British politics at the moment is that all
sorts of groups are fighting rearguard actions against
emerging, alternative political models. The old models no
longer serve us well, but such is our nostalgia for ancient
institutions in this country that we would rather perish
with the old than flourish with the new. We are left with
institutions in Church and State that consume all our ener-
gies and prevent us from contemplating new possibilities.
In the case of the Church, our understandable affection
for our buildings is paralleled in the way we organize
ourselves into pastoral units. We have long since ceased
to be a gathering people, a people on the move through
history. We have become a gathered people, settled on a
high beach, where we manage and embellish the life we
have created for ourselves.

The problem here is that the structures we have evolved
to express the Gospel of God's Grace and our access to it
have done their work too well. Our need to objectify the
divine has led us to set aside categories of persons and
places, times and substances as particular means through
which Grace can operate. We have ended by associating
the divine exclusively with these instrumentalities. We
have forgotten the admonition to flee from idols; we have
ignored God's anxiety about being locked into a house
made of cedar. We have created our own golden calves.

For example, specific forms of Godtalk, of theology, have become idols. Forms of language that were meant to stimulate and provoke thought, metaphors that were to shock and challenge, have themselves become fixed objects we spend our energy protecting. The word 'metaphor' means to carry over from one reality and apply it to another, thereby provoking insight and understanding. It is a figure of speech. All theology is metaphorical. It is the way we seek to express the inexpressible, to utter the unutterable, to eff the ineffable. God comes *through* it, though God is not limited to it, but our passion for objectification makes idols of our propositions and formulas. This is why there is so much passion and outrage on both sides of the debate about what is allowable language in our rites of worship. Those who say that only their metaphors offer true access to God make Godtalk more important than Godself.

Obviously, metaphors will vary. Some will be more useful, more enduring than others, more apt, more able to create sudden sparks of insight; but the system itself is contingent upon the originating reality of God whose spirit blows where it will and can make the very rustling of the olive leaves convey mystery to us.

I think I can best sum up what I've been trying to say by recounting an experience I had at Taizé some years ago. I was invited to visit Taizé by Brother Roger and I prepared for my first encounter with the Community with great excitement. The thing I was most looking forward to was taking part in the Taizé Office. I had used that Office Book in the early 1970s and remembered its richness and diversity. In creating their form of prayer, the brothers had borrowed from the great monastic traditions and had achieved a remarkable work of liturgical art. The Taizé Office Book followed the Christian year with a suitably embroidered richness of expression. I looked forward to sitting in the chapel at Taizé and listening to the white-cowled brothers singing their elaborate office in impeccable Gelineau chants. It was in that mood that I went to evening prayer on my first day at Taizé. The place was packed with young people from all over the world. I noticed that they'd knocked one of the walls out of the great church they had built for the Community, and added a tent-like structure to it, to accommodate more people. The Office itself was not what I expected. I was deeply moved by it, but I was intrigued by its simplicity: some chants, a few verses of scripture read in six or seven different languages, a psalm, and a long period of silence. At supper with the brothers after the evening office, I asked them about their form of prayer. What had happened to the Taizé Office Book? 'Ah, yes,' they said, 'we still have it, of course. Indeed, we are proud of it. But God started sending all these young people to us from all over the world and it was quite obvious that the form of prayer we had developed for ourselves was not appropriate to these new circumstances, so we abandoned it. Everything is provisional, you know. Only God is God.'

The power of the provisional, the doctrine of provisionality, is a profoundly important and liberating one, which rescues us from all the idolatries that are the great enemy of God. Scripture is full of images that make the same point. It describes the life of faith as a journey through a wilderness and believers as pioneers, not settlers in permanent communities with houses built on fixed foundations. God is always up ahead of us, leading us on through history, inviting us to discover the divine in our own contemporary experience. I think this is a particular challenge for the Church of England, which has inherited so many wonderful old buildings and a marvellous old liturgy. It becomes difficult to resist the notion that God's most significant activity has been somewhere back in the past and that it is the duty of the Church to preserve what God has done rather than identify what God is doing. So the Church becomes the spiritual arm of the National Trust, part of the heritage industry, there to preserve and conserve what has been, never ever to be concerned with what may be coming to pass. This theory of Christianity traps us in the past, but the doctrine of provisionality, if we will let it, will rescue us from this idolatrizing nostalgia and will enable us to reverence and appropriate the past without idolatrizing it and give us the courage and expectance to discern God's action today.

It is sometimes asserted that everything that has developed in Christianity, particularly in Catholic Christianity, was implicit in the New Testament from the very beginning. This conviction is often described as the organic model. The full flowering of Catholic Christianity is the oak tree which came from the acorn, the Christ event, the originating fact of Christianity, from which everything else has organically grown. While suggestive and helpful as far as it goes, I find the organic model of Christianity limiting and not totally persuasive. It suggests a picture of a community going out from the beginning with a fixed message and a fixed structure, however implicit.

That was only ever half the truth. In a crucial verse in John 16, Christ tells us that God's revelatory activity will never be over. God, he tells us, has new things to teach us that we cannot hear now, but the Holy Spirit will guide us into an understanding of them. The main energy of the New Testament is the energy of movement and discovery. It paints a picture of a God who comes, not a God who has already been. Scripture tells us to look for this God, expect to find this God, not only in the midst of the licensed assemblies of faith but at the edges, on the margins. It is the Syro-Phoenician woman, the outsider, who challenges Jesus and his disciples to share the message of God's love with Gentiles as well as with Jews. It is the Roman non-commissioned officer Cornelius, another outsider, whom God uses to persuade Peter that the Christian gospel was for all and not just for his cousins in Jerusalem.

What are the implications of this dynamic element in the Christian tradition? It would seem to me that the main implication is that God will be trying to tell the Church something new, and God will be speaking to it from its own edges and from the edges of society. One of the things that seems to be happening in our society is that new political models are being born. The new models are models of community, models that emphasize plurality and mutuality, and the ability of all men and women to play their part in finding structures appropriate to their needs. The old, male-dominated, verticalized, centralized, highly concentrated institution will increasingly be a thing of the past. It alienates people, makes them dependent.

Just as the old Church could not but model itself on vertical structures, so today's Church should learn from these new emerging horizontal structures. We should sit more lightly to the institutional model we have inherited and experiment with more human models, models of co-operation that emphasize the plural nature of humanity. If we followed this approach, then the Church's ministry would not be there to rule but to stimulate, to encourage creativity. We would be the poets and clowns, not the managing directors of the new people of God, and the Church we operated within would be open at the edges. It would be a Church that reflected the untidy reality of faith-seeking and faith-sharing. Church membership would be an invitation to pilgrimage, an invitation to accompany a people on the way, not enrolment in an institution on a fixed site. If the Church followed this new model, there would be radical experiments in Christian living, in liturgy and prayer, in theological exploration, in faith-sharing and prophetic witness. We might retain our buildings but they would be resources from which we went out, rather than places into which we insisted on drawing people. Our buildings, too, would be less static in feel and layout. They would reflect the living reality of God towards whom we are being drawn. They would be places where silence was a powerful reality as well as creativity; and our clergy would be as famous for their ability to shut up as they are for speaking out. The Church would reflect the reality of God, who's not old and wearing out like some of us, but endlessly new, full of surprises, calling us to follow in trust into the great future that awaits us.

I'm not suggesting that we should necessarily scrap the forms and structures of Christianity as we have received them. I *am* saying that we should recognize them for what they are, maybe for the first time. They are all provisional, all relative. Establishment, ministry, ecclesial structures, theological methods are all temporary instruments that inevitably reach their use-by date. If we cling to them beyond that they become idols. It is important to know and name the idol in our life, in the Church and in the nation, whether it is an economic theory that bloats the already rich and demeans the already poor, or a doctrine of ministry that limits the action of God and sets boundaries upon God's grace. We should name it, challenge it and seek to overturn it, because only God deserves our absolute loyalty. Only God is God, and it is only God's service that is perfect freedom.

I have a strong sense that most of the religious structures and many of the secular structures in our country are at a moment of crisis that can lead either to renewal or terminal decay. I think this is something of what David Jenkins means when he talks about the dark night of our institutions. It is no accident that in these anxious and uncertain times fundamentalisms grow like weeds and religions of hate and exclusion multiply. These are idolatries, objectivications of our own fears, they are not the way forward. I am not exactly sure what the way is. I only know that it has to be a way out and not a way back. Ours is a God who is ahead of us, preparing places for us, going before us. It has always been a frightening thing to follow the God who wants to liberate us from the consolations of our slavery to idols. When the children of Israel, against their better judgement, followed Moses out of Egypt they saw that the Egyptians were marching after them and we are told that they were in great fear:

> And the people of Israel cried out to the Lord; and they said to Moses, 'Is it because there are no graves in Egypt that you have taken us away to die in the wilderness? What have you done to us in bringing us out of Egypt? Is not this what we said to you in Egypt, let us alone and let us serve the Egyptians? For it would have been better for us to serve the Egyptians than to die in the wilderness.'

141

> And Moses said to the people, 'Fear not, stand firm, and see the salvation of the Lord, which he will work for you today; for the Egyptians whom you see today you shall never see again. The Lord will fight for you, and you have only to be still.'
>
> The Lord said to Moses, 'Why do you cry to me? Tell the people of Israel to go forward.'

Tell the people to go forward, forward in faith.

8 Sermon given in York Minster, 5 September 1993*

Frank T. Griswold

A Franciscan priest I know tells the story of his visit some years ago to the formidable pioneer of modern mental health, Dr Karl Menninger. Having entered the great man's presence, the priest, searching for a topic worthy of pursuit, asked Dr Menninger what, in his opinion, based upon his many years of experience, was the primary cause of mental illness. Dr Menninger paused and thought for a moment and slowly replied that the cause was not genetic, or traumatic, but was to be found in one's inability to forgive – the inability to forgive ourselves for being imperfect.

As I reflected upon Dr Menninger's words after hearing that story, I knew that they were true, certainly true of me, and I then remembered an occasion when, several years earlier, I had been moved at the end of a week's retreat at a Benedictine monastery in upstate New York, to make what I thought would be the most thorough and searching confession of my life. (I was in my early 40s and had been making my confession regularly since the age of 15). I should have known something was awry when, *en route* to the appointment, I began to reflect on how thorough I had been in my self-examination. No corner of my soul had gone unexamined; no closet door within my heart had gone unopened. This is going to be a dazzling display of self-scrutiny and self-accusation. No

*© Frank T. Griswold 1993

doubt my confessor (who knew me well) will be very impressed indeed.'

The moment came and we sat facing one another in the small parlour used for such encounters, as I poured forth the dark fruits of my penitential labours. I finished and I waited, wondering if my monkish friend had ever before encountered such acuity of self-expressed sinfulness. And then he did something I was completely unprepared for: he smiled and said quietly, 'Frank, welcome to the human condition.' Then leaning forward, he added, 'You don't have to be so hard on yourself.'

In that moment, what I had hoped to be relieved of through the sacramental rite of reconciliation was given back to me: my imperfect self, my limitations and deficiencies, my inescapable and troublesome and all too human 'Frankness'. But something else, something far more important, was given as well, something which allowed me not only to take back, but to welcome and to embrace those dimensions of my self which I had sought to judge and condemn. And what was that something else I was given? It was Christ's welcoming mercy and quick-eyed love made flesh, made real, made obvious and inescapable in the very human smile and words of the fellow Christian, the fellow limb of Christ's risen body, the fellow recipient of that same mercy, who sat smiling before me.

And why do I tell you this tale? I do so because it is a way of gathering up and weaving together and celebrating many of the things a number of us who are here this morning have been naming and holding up and reflecting upon during these past four days at a conference held at the University of York on the future of the Catholic tradition within our Anglican household.

The tale I have told you is not primarily about me: it is about tradition becoming the means whereby one is able to move forward, from self-deception into truth, from bondage to freedom. It is about the power of the sacraments to convey the Gospel and to make Jesus' story and our story one; it is about mercy made flesh; it is about healing; it is about discovering personhood; it is about being grasped and re-grasped by the liberating, lifegiving, generous, ever-enlarging, robust and spacious fullness of God. In short, it is about being overtaken, caught off guard and surprised by the fierce fullness of God's love fitted, with gentle humour, to our fragile capacities to receive and welcome it. It is a tale about God's Catholicity, God's own wholeness dwelling among us as a gift to be received and as a life to be lived, and not as some sort of abstract position which will allow us to offset our imperfections, or separate ourselves in the name of some narrow orthodoxy from the Gospel experiences of others.

'I feel a great call to help on the renewal of sane Catholicism in England and am sure it is a work of God.' Possibly the Warden of Pleshey Retreat House will recognize these words; they come from Evelyn Underhill and were written in 1933. This great call is still valid 60 years later and now it is your call as well, and yet it must be clearly said that a sane (and sensible as well as critical) Catholicism can become an illusion, a potential excursion into self-deception, a fantasy, unless it is first and foremost a *humble* and *prayerful* Catholicism, a Catholicism which, after the example of Mary of Nazareth (and unashamedly supported by her prayers), listens with an open, expectant, and undefended heart to God's word in the very circumstances of our lives, and the struggles and the yearnings of the world around us.

This morning's readings (Ephesians 5:25–6:4; Mark 10:2–16) set before us the profound relationship of mutual listening and awareness realized and made flesh in the bond between husband and wife in marriage . . . marriage not seen as free-standing, but pointing beyond itself to Christ and Christ's relationship to his own Body, the Church. Just as a husband is called to love his wife as he does his own body, so Christ loves his own body, that is each one of us, distinctly, personally and in relation to one another: 'Husbands, love your wives, just as Christ loved the Church and gave himself up for her in order to make her holy' (Ephesians 5:25–26). And what is holiness?

145

Holiness happens to us; it comes upon us, it overrules us and refuses to serve our own ends. Remember how the Lord overruled Paul's ego ideal: his longing to be set free from the thorn in his flesh which confronted him constantly with his own imperfections. 'Three times I appealed to the Lord about this, that it would leave me, but he said to me, "My grace is sufficient for you, for power is made perfect in weakness" ' (2 Corinthians 12:8–9).

Holiness is God's wholeness revealed in the midst of our weakness: it transforms us by setting us free from self-preoccupation and self-judgement and shame. Our wounds, our imperfections, may remain but they are caught up into Christ and become part of the continuous unfolding of Christ's story in us. This process of being grasped and caught up and transformed in Christ is wonderfully described by Symeon the New Theologian:

> We awaken in Christ's body
> as Christ awakens our bodies,
> and my poor hand is Christ, He enters
> my foot, and is infinitely me.
>
> I move my hand, and wonderfully
> my hand becomes Christ, becomes all of Him
> (God is indivisibly
> whole, seamless in His Godhood).
>
> I move my foot, and at once
> He appears like a flash of lightning.
> Do my words seem blasphemous? – Then
> open your heart to Him
>
> and let yourself receive the one
> who is opening to you so deeply.
> For if we genuinely love Him,
> we wake up inside Christ's body
>
> where all our body, all over,
> every most hidden part of it,
> is realized in joy as Him,
> and He makes us, utterly, real,

and everything that is hurt, everything
that seemed to us dark, harsh, shameful,
maimed, ugly, irreparably
damaged, is in Him transformed

and recognized as whole, as lovely,
and radiant in His light
we awaken as the Beloved
in every last part of our body.

Here once again we are confronted by God's Catholicity, God's fullness worked in us by Christ in order that we might waken as the Beloved, as Christ himself, *in every last part of our body*.

This wonderful vision of incarnation, of our bodies transformed and thereby revealing the radiant light of God's mercy, is a vision and not just of us individually but of all of us together; it is a vision of the Church, a Church which is bold and imaginative and adventurous, a Church which embodies the fullness of God's love as justice and compassion in the flesh of its members, a Church which, in union with the Beloved, is able to produce leaves for the healing of the nations.

In a few moments the risen Christ will meet us with quick-eyed love in the Eucharistic feast in order to renew, enlarge, and extend our union with him and with one another for the sake of the world. Let us, therefore, heed the words of Symeon: 'Open your hearts to him, and let yourself receive the one who is opening to you so deeply.' But as we go forth from this encounter, this meeting in bread and wine, let us also hear the insistent whisper of Christ deep within us: 'I offer you freedom of life in all its fullness, and now – surprise me.'

Amen.

Note on
Affirming Catholicism

Affirming Catholicism has never been and is not intended to be yet another 'party' within the Church of England or the Anglican Communion.

Following the first national conference in York in July 1991, a successful application was lodged with the Charity Commissioners for charitable status for Affirming Catholicism and its publishing outlet, *Mainstream*. The following is extracted from the Trust Deed:

> It is the conviction of many that a respect for scholarship and free enquiry has been characteristic of the Church of England and of the Churches of the wider Anglican Communion from earliest times and is fully consistent with the status of those Churches as part of the Holy Catholic Church. It is desired to establish a charitable educational foundation which will be true both to those characteristics and to the Catholic tradition within Anglicanism . . .
>
> . . . The object of the foundation shall be the advancement of education in the doctrines and the historical development of the Church of England and the Churches of the wider Anglican Communion, as held by those professing to stand within the Catholic tradition.
>
> The intention is:
>
> 1. To organise or support lectures, conferences and seminars.
>
> 2. To publish or support books, tracts, journals and other educational material.
>
> 3. To provide resources for local groups of supporters of the foundation meeting for purposes of study and discussion.

The Steering Committee consists of:

Mr Lewis Ayres
The Revd Dr Lida Ellsworth
The Revd Preb. John Gaskell
The Most Revd Richard Holloway
The Revd David Hutt
The Revd Dr Jeffrey John
The Revd Nerissa Jones
Mr Martin Lawrence
The Very Revd Dr John Moses
The Rt Revd Jack Nicholls
The Revd June Osborne
The Revd Victor Stock
Angela Tilby
Dame Rachel Waterhouse
The Rt Revd Rowan Williams

Enquiries regarding the aims and activities of Affirming Catholicism together with its publications and future programme may be addressed to:

Elizabeth Field
Affirming Catholicism
St Mary-le-Bow
Cheapside
London EC2V 6AU